WAITING AT THE ALTAR

Is Christ delayed, or are we?

BY

SHAWN BRACE

TEACH Services, Inc.
Brushton, New York

2008 09 10 11 12 · 5 4 3 2 1

Copyright © 2008 TEACH Services, Inc.
ISBN-13: 978-1-57258-536-2
ISBN-10: 1-57258-536-6
Library of Congress Control Number: 2008902628

Published by

TEACH Services, Inc.
www.TEACHServices.com

Contents

ACKNOWLEDGMENTS

This book would not be possible without the patient love of my wife. Something of this magnitude does not get written unless she is willing to take a back seat at times. I can't even begin to count the number of times I would come home from my classes in the seminary, and quickly run to my computer to pump out a few more pages. She also provided helpful feedback as each chapter was being written.

I also want to thank Wanda Hopkins, my aunt, who proofread the entire manuscript as well, editing my poor grammar and providing much needed insight. She has always inspired me to write, and her support has always uplifted me tremendously.

The rest of my family has always been supportive as well, and in many ways, my parents, brother and sister, brother-in-law, my little niece Calleigh, as well as cousins, aunts and uncles, and grandmother, have all been instrumental in this book. It is with you all in mind that I have written this book. I hope you take these ideas to heart and give them some good thought. Heaven awaits us.

It would also be remiss of me not to mention the wonderful relationships I enjoyed at Andrews University, especially during my seminary training. The Grounds Department, first of all, provided me with ample opportunity to formulate my thoughts as I mowed lawns or shoveled snow. Many a chapter was written as I went about my tasks. Thus, the reason the grass looked so poor after I was done. Sorry! Also, my seminary colleagues who I worked with on grounds—particularly Kyle Baldwin and Jeff Steinke—whose ears I talked off with ideas for this book. Thanks for listening and helping me tighten my ideas.

I would also like to especially thank those who supported me financially toward the goal of writing this book and getting it published. I don't even know who all of you are, but I am greatly indebted to you for helping me pursue this endeavor. Your giving will not soon be forgotten.

Most importantly, I would like to thank God, who has been ever patient with me. Thank You for giving me the ability, I believe, to write somewhat clearly and explain truths that matter most to You. Please continue to touch my heart with Your compassion. And thanks for inviting me to the grandest wedding that will ever take place. Hopefully we'll all show up soon.

Not often does the publishing world get a book that blows right by the thousands published at the same time. In these pages, Shawn answers the question that most every theologian avoids or waffles on. That question is the most significant question that ever could be asked: What does God want to accomplish in His Plan of Salvation?

Shawn simply lets the biblical story unfold the answer. He permits John the Revelator to set the stage for the most majestic wedding in the universe—the day when God's Salvation Plan is consummated. What Hollywood producer/director could ever come close to the drama John describes in the nineteenth chapter of the book of Revelation!

Guests without number look on—banks of angels on cue, singing the wedding processional: "Alleluia! For the Lord God Omnipotent reigns! Let us be glad and rejoice and give Him glory, for the marriage of the Lamb [Jesus] has come, and His wife has made herself ready." Unfallen worlds of created intelligences stand as witnesses to the rightness of the wedding vows, vouching for the integrity of all parties concerned—"True and righteous are His judgments!"

The incredible part of this wedding is that the unfallen worlds and innumerable angels have been waiting for a long time for the bride to show up! Any way we look at this delayed wedding, it has to be astonishing! How can this be? The Lord Jesus waiting at the altar! The Lord Omnipotent, the Lord of time and space, waiting!

Who is He waiting for? Waiting for the final generation of His professed followers to make up their minds. About what? Whether they really want to follow Him wherever He leads! Whether they have so settled themselves into their loyalty to Him that they will never be moved by any wooing from any other suitor!

But John through his prophetic eye sees the day when our Lord's bride "made herself ready!" Though the Groom

3

is Lord of time and space, the Omnipotent One—there is something even He can not do! He can not make His bride ready for the wedding!

With unusual clarity and winsomeness, our author tells this story for which all the universe is waiting. This wedding is the answer to the greatest question that can be asked: What does God want to accomplish in His Plan of Salvation? Every one of us is part of that answer! The Plan of Salvation is accomplished when men and women say *yes* to whatever God wants for their happiness. And that *yes* gets so settled into their neural patterns that they will never be moved ever again to say *no* to God, ever! That's when our Lord Jesus says to the universe, "Here is my bride—she is safe to marry!"

January 1, 2008
Herbert Edgar Douglass
Lincoln Hills, California

FOR MY DAD

*You have taught and shown me
more about my heavenly Father
than you'll ever know.*

SECTION ONE

THE DELAYED WEDDING

CHAPTER 1

Call me crazy, and I know you will, but I love being a Seventh-day Adventist. Absolutely love it. I love the sense of community the church brings. I love Sabbath afternoon hikes. I love campmeeting. I love our educational system. I love that satisfying feeling I get when I hear a mission story in Sabbath School, realizing I contributed my four dollars in last month's offering to make that story possible. I love the *idea* behind a "haystack" (although you must have the right kind of chips and beans to make me happy). I love hearing the reports of the thousands of baptisms in some third world country and how much the church is growing. I love a good sermon that leaves me with a warm feeling inside. I love the fact that there are Seventh-day Adventists in 206 countries around the world. And boy, do I love to hear the congregation sing a good, hearty hymn at the end of a church service. I love it.

I love it all.

Actually, I love it so much that I think I would be more than content to live like this for the rest of my life. Who needs heaven when you can enjoy such a great life here on earth? As long as membership continues to grow at a rapid pace, tithe is up, and the world is in a fairly good state, I could live like this forever.

But then something hit me. I'm a Seventh-day *Adventist*, not just a Seventh-day Christian. Not only do I believe that Jesus is coming, but my name implies that I believe He's coming *soon*. The dictionary tells me the word "adventist" means that I believe in the "imminent advent of Christ." *Imminent*, meaning like, *soon*; believing it is "about to occur."

We've been singing the song, "Soon and very soon, we are going to see the King" for over 160 years now. Apparently the word "soon" is relative though; 160 years is a very short time when you look at the big picture and the 6000-year-old earth.

We could have many more years left yet and, in the words of the great New England poet, Robert Frost, "miles to go before we sleep."

But something just isn't adding up to me. Every major event that takes place in the world seems to signal the definite return of Jesus. They, many times, leave no questions in our minds. "Oh, the Lord cannot linger very much longer; He must be coming soon," we say. "The world is just getting worse and worse."

We've been saying that for years now, but the good Lord still hasn't returned.

William Miller and his followers were convinced the Lord was coming in 1844. Ellen White said that "if all who had labored unitedly in the work of 1844 had received the third angel's message and proclaimed it in the power of the Holy Spirit...Christ would have come for the redemption of His people."[1] She said that in 1893.

I'm sure the World Wars brought forth these same thoughts to many Christians and Seventh-day Adventists alike. My grandmother said that God would never let man walk on the moon. You should have seen the look on my face when I was eight years old and I heard that the United States had just bombed Baghdad. And I'm sure that September 11 is still fresh in all of our minds, never mind Hurricane Katrina, Tina, and all the other natural disasters that seem to strike our world every other week. Each of these events brought thoughts of Christ's soon return to the forefront of our minds.

Yet, here we are. Still. The wait continues.

What's going on with God up there? Has He forgotten about us? Perhaps the heavenly vehicles have broken down and need repair, or gasoline prices have skyrocketed in heaven, too.

We may as well buckle down and prepare ourselves to wait this one out. It may be a while yet.

But could we be missing something?

Sad as it may seem, many people are tired of hearing this "Jesus is coming soon" banter. In fact, I recently heard of a Sabbath School teacher who was approached by a number of families in her class, requesting she not mention anything about Jesus' Second Coming anymore. Apparently, the idea is too passé.

But, occasionally, there are a few people who do tackle the issue of Christ's apparent delay. While most people just shrug it off and say, "I don't know. I'm not worried about it. He'll come when He comes," a few are genuinely concerned about why it has taken Him so long.

And we should be concerned. Not only do we look stupid to the world, since we proclaim the message that Jesus is coming soon, but more importantly, it makes *God* look stupid to the world. After all, He proclaimed, "I am coming soon," numerous times in the Bible, and His death was for the purpose of returning to earth and claiming His people for whom He died. Thus, it makes Christ's death unnecessary if there is no Second Coming. You can see how serious the implications are.

Perhaps a number of people are not Christians simply because Jesus proclaimed this 2000 years ago and still hasn't come. To many, He's nothing but a liar, if He even exists.

Yet we show little concern for Jesus' reputation and just shrug it off, more concerned with our personal status and image. It is refreshing, though, when people do face the issue. But I'm afraid many of us are lost when it comes to an answer that truly makes sense.

One reason we give for Christ's delay is that Jesus is waiting as long as possible for that "one last person" to make a decision to follow Him. He knows there is just *one* person whose decision is hanging in the balance. But this reasoning just doesn't add up to me.

At that rate Christ would *never* come.

I don't know what the statistics are, but every minute that goes by, thousands of babies are born into the world. The longer God waits, the more people will have to make a decision for Him, and on and on it could go. It could turn into an endless cycle of waiting. The world would go on forever without the return of Christ.

Another reason we like to give is that God's heavenly clock just hasn't struck twelve yet. Earth's history is in its eleventh hour, we like to say, just minutes away from striking midnight, when Christ will finally return.

Is this to say, then, that God picked some random date out of a hat thousands of years ago, deciding to come on that exact date, regardless of what state the world was in? This idea doesn't seem to go along with God's character. He never does anything arbitrarily and has a reason for everything He does. This explanation seems to stem from the Calvinistic idea of predestination, where God works independently of any other external circumstances because of His sovereignty.

If this were the case too, who's to say that the arbitrary date He picked isn't really hundreds of years away still? Besides, Jesus clearly tells us, "But of that day and hour, no one knows, not even the angels in heaven, nor the Son" (Mark 13:32). Imagine if Christ returned and only *one* person was prepared to meet Him. Sure, Christ would be excited about that one person, but it would be somewhat of an embarrassing situation. What an anti-climactic return it would be. Perhaps this is why the book of Revelation quotes God as saying, "Thrust in Your sickle and reap, for the time has come for You to reap, for the harvest of the earth is ripe" (Revelation 14:15). This seems to indicate that the condition of the harvest has something to do with the timing of Christ's return.

So the question still stands: Where's God and what is He doing?

I like to tell people that after 11 million, 520 thousand minutes of waiting, I *finally* got a girlfriend. That's right, for the first 8,000 days of my life—or roughly 22 and a half years—I was without a significant other.

And people knew it. Although I committed this area of my life to Christ and wanted Him to lead out in every facet of it, I was anxious about finding a nice young lady. It seemed as though it was all I could talk about, think about, dream about, and live about. I wanted to find an awesome girl. And I did.

Fortunately, God finally blessed me and I started dating—and then married—this wonderful young lady after being friends with her for quite a number of years.

But before we started dating, we almost met disaster.

You see, before Camille and I started dating, we were at different colleges; she in Texas and I in Michigan. As you can imagine, our deepening friendship was, to a large degree, established over the telephone. After spending the summer together working at camp in Maine, we parted ways and immediately began calling one another, writing letters, e-mailing each other (about three times a day), and using any other form of communication we could find.

Ever prayerful about the friendship, I wanted to make sure that God was leading in our relationship and that I was not running ahead of His timing. This is especially difficult to do when dozens of people are constantly asking you what the status of your relationship is, including a mother whose greatest desire is for her son to get a girlfriend and ultimately get married. But for a significant period of time, I didn't feel as if God was leading me forward.

And then the time came. Having prayed about the relationship for some time, and seeking the counsel of older, wiser people, I felt impressed that I needed to talk with the young lady about our friendship. After calling her dad and sharing my intentions with him, I called her and shared my thoughts with her.

Fortunately, the feelings were mutual. But the issue was complicated because we were, for all practical purposes, worlds apart physically. We didn't think that our relationship should start long distance, but we weren't sure if God wanted us together at that time.

So we decided to take a five-day break from one another, individually praying that God would show us what He desired for our relationship. This meant that we wouldn't call each other, e-mail each other, send letters via Carrier Pigeon...nothing.

As you can imagine, it was a long five days, full of anticipation. A million things went through my mind about our relationship and what God wanted us to do. But when the fifth day arrived, I was excited about answering the phone when she was finally going to call.

She never called though. As the evening came and darkness approached, I nervously sat in my dorm room. Although I wasn't waiting *right* by the phone, it was definitely in close proximity.

What is going on? I wondered. Was she too scared to call me? Did she forget my number? Or worse yet, did she want nothing to do with me anymore? A million scenarios ran through my mind, and I didn't like the sound of any of them.

Fortunately, God intervened. I happened to be chatting with a mutual friend of ours online, and when I mentioned to her how I was looking forward to my conversation with Camille, the friend replied, "Oh, yeah, I was talking with Camille earlier, and she was excited that you were calling her tonight."

"Wait a minute!" I replied. "*I'm* supposed to call *her*?"

Apparently, something had been lost in the translation between Camille and me during our previous conversation (imagine that—a male and female having a misunderstanding!): I had the impression that she was calling me, and she had the impression that I was calling her.

So once that misunderstanding was quickly averted, I picked up the phone and dialed the number, and the rest is history.

But imagine what would have happened had neither of us called. Who knows what we would have thought. Who knows what the ramifications would have been; all because I was sitting there waiting for her, not realizing that the whole time she was waiting for *me*.

And I am left wondering: could we be sitting here on earth waiting for God to return, not realizing that the whole time He is actually waiting for *us*? Could it be? Maybe the price of gas in heaven isn't all that high. Maybe the heavenly vehicles haven't broken down. Maybe God's clock has already struck twelve, and we're now in sudden death overtime.

Maybe, just maybe, we're not waiting for God. Maybe He's waiting for us.

NOTES

1. Ellen White, *Review and Herald Extra*, Feb. 28, 1893.

CHAPTER II

Perhaps you are skeptical about the ideas I have proposed so far. The idea that there is a delay in Christ's Second Coming may seem absurd to some, while others may find it even more troubling that Christ is waiting on us, rather than the other way around. If this is what you are thinking, that's fine. We don't have to be enemies over it. I'm just going to try and convince you otherwise.

Thus, a burning question must be confronted before delving into the rest of the book: Is there *really* a delay in Christ's Second Coming? Or is this simply a figment of some people's imagination, particularly mine?

Right from the beginning some people may object that God isn't constrained to time. After all, 2 Peter 3:8 says that "with the Lord one day is as a thousand years and a thousand years as one day." God is not limited by time, we reason, and therefore not subjected to our measurements of it.

The truth is, however, the same God who stands outside of time also created it and has chosen to reveal Himself to human beings within its limits. Quite simply, He wouldn't interact with us through time on one front, but then when it comes to His Second Coming stand back and say, "Oh, but time doesn't really apply to Me; so the timing of my return is irrelevant."

God is acutely aware of the timing of His return. He eagerly awaits it and urges us to do the same.

The importance of time surely resonates when anticipating a soon-coming wedding. This was brought home to me the few months before my much anticipated wedding day. And when I say that it was much anticipated, we're talking anticipation that was building up in my mind since the time I was separated from my mother at birth. (I have never been a typical guy.)

About a month before my "big day," I was attending the required camp pitch for all the conference pastors.

17

Unfortunately, speaking of time, I was a little late to the first meeting, and as I walked into the gathering, the conference president—who was making various introductions—saw me and yelled out, "How many days until your wedding?" Without missing a beat, I replied, "22 days." Needless to say, all of my colleagues were impressed with my precise calculations.

In fact, the conference secretary was so impressed that every time I saw him for the next two weeks he had one question for me: "How many days?" Even if he had seen me the previous day and asked me the same question, he would still ask, "How many days?" as if the number weren't one less than the day before.

Do you think the precise calculation of my anticipated wedding day was important to me? Of course it was! And don't you think I would have been greatly troubled if the wedding day had been delayed for a few days, weeks, months, or years?

To be honest with you, there came a point in my engagement when I actually sat down and calculated how many days I had left until my wedding day. This is the reason I could tell my conference president how many days I had left until my wedding with confidence. I was counting down the days with great anticipation.

Incidentally, God did the same thing. Although there are many different time prophecies on His heavenly calendar, none is greater than the one He revealed in Daniel 8:14. There we read, "For two thousand three hundred days; then the sanctuary shall be cleansed." This, of course, refers to Christ's High Priestly ministry in the Most Holy Place of the heavenly sanctuary.

Even more specifically, however, this 2300-day time prophecy refers to the beginning of His wedding day in 1844.

The reason I can say this is because of the antitypical fulfillment of the Jewish festivals that took place during their calendar year. I know the word "antitypical" is a big word, but it carries a simple meaning. The dictionary defines an antitype as "one that is foreshadowed by or identified with an earlier symbol or type." Therefore, the symbols in the Old Testament were simply "sneak previews" of greater truths that were to take place and meet their fulfillment in Christ.

This is vividly seen in the yearly festivals that the Israelites observed throughout the year. We've all heard of Passover and Pentecost, and we may even be familiar with the Day of Atonement and the Feast of Tabernacles. These were all holidays (or, literally "Holy Days") for the Jewish people.

Much like our modern holidays, in which we commemorate certain events that have happened in history, these festivals were to remind the Israelites of God's deliverance in the past. In the United States, for example, we celebrate Martin Luther King, Jr. Day. This holiday points back to the tremendous work that Martin Luther King did within the Civil Rights Movement. We also celebrate Independence Day on July 4, remembering the courage of our forefathers in declaring independence from Britain.

This is precisely what many of the Jewish festivals did. They pointed back to God's deliverance and reminded the Israelites of His constant care and protection for them. This is clearly seen in Passover, which reminded the Israelites of how God had liberated them from Egypt.

But the festivals pointed to more than just the past. They also pointed to the future, when they would have a grander fulfillment with the Messiah's coming.

The neat thing about history is that we can look back and see how these festivals met their fulfillment. In sequential order, each of the yearly festivals have been fulfilled or are about to be fulfilled. Passover, for example, which was the first major festival in the Jewish year, was fulfilled at Calvary when Christ shed His blood for the alienated world. Not only was this fulfilled antitypically, but, as you may recall, the crucifixion did literally take place on Passover weekend.

The next major Jewish festival, which was Pentecost, also saw its antitypical fulfillment in the "Upper Room" with the early apostles. The book of Acts tells us that "when the Day of Pentecost had fully come" the apostles were in one place and became "filled with the Holy Spirit and began to speak with other tongues" (Acts 2:1, 4). Pentecost was celebrated like never before.

Not all of the festivals have met their antitypical fulfillment yet, however. The last festival of the Jewish calendar year is still a future promise. This last festival, commonly known as the "Feast of Tabernacles" or the "Feast of Booths," will reach its full meaning in the New Jerusalem. Just as the ancient Israelites were to prepare booths to live in during this festival, so will all of God's people live in booths—or mansions, or houses, or shacks—in the New Jerusalem. It will be the grandest festival of all.

But the Feast of Tabernacles didn't take place until another holiday finished. That holiday, as you may be well aware, was the Day of Atonement. Thus, before the New Jerusalem comes the Day of Atonement. It just so happens, of course, that Daniel 8:14 tells us that we are now living during this time period.

I know that you didn't pick up this book to fill in cute little charts that make you add and subtract years and remind you of the year zero (or the lack thereof), but it is paramount to understand that this cosmic Day of Atonement began in 1844.

Incidentally, after this 2300-day time prophecy, there are no other time prophecies in the Bible that still need to be fulfilled. This is the longest time prophecy in the Bible. Much like a wedding checklist that signifies different deadlines for different components of a wedding (i.e., the flowers need to be ordered three weeks before the wedding, or the photographer needs to be confirmed three days before), the 2300-day prophecy in Daniel is the last and final deadline that the Bible gives. You can scour its pages for another deadline that moves beyond 1844, but there isn't one.

This is why, when Daniel sat perplexed about this prophecy, an angel appeared to him and said, "Understand, son of man, that the vision refers to the time of the end" (Daniel 8:17).

In a way, then, this prophecy tells us that Christ's wedding has already started. Ever since 1844 God has been in the Most Holy Place—the marriage room of heaven— waiting for His bride to show up there and join Him at the altar. Only after she shows up and the "I dos" are said can the honeymoon, in which they enjoy the ultimate Feast of Tabernacles in the mansions on high, take place.

So it stands to reason: Could Christ not have come at any point after October 22, 1844? Truthfully, couldn't He have come on October *23*? After all, it doesn't take an almighty, all-powerful God 160 plus years to go about His work in the Most Holy Place of the heavenly sanctuary. The same God who created this entire planet in seven shorts days could go about this work just as quickly, if not faster.

It leads me to believe that perhaps, after all, there has been a delay in His return. Maybe Christ could have truly come at any point after 1844. He is, no doubt, the most anxious Groom the universe has ever seen, eager to take His bride's hand in marriage as soon as He can.

Something must be holding Him up.

CHAPTER III

BEWARE OF THE BRIDEZILLA

Grooms and future grooms, beware: There are potential "Bridezillas" lurking among us. Do you know what I'm talking about? These are brides who get downright nasty about preparing for their wedding. As one author put it, Bridezillas are women who "terrorize their bridal party and family members, make greedy demands, and break all rules of etiquette, to ensure that they are the single most important person on the planet from the time they are engaged to the time they are married."[1] I was alerted to this phenomenon in the months that led up to my own wedding, though not as a result of my bride's behavior.

When you're a soon-to-be-married man, your senses are heightened to wedding talk. Indeed, it seems to be the topic of conversation with everyone you come in contact with. ("Oh, your leg just fell off? Say, how are the wedding plans coming along?") People—usually women—you've never even seen before come up to you and ask about the upcoming wedding. Needless to say, it's at the forefront of your cerebral cortex.

Thus, while flipping through the TV channels one day as I was home for lunch, I noticed a show that was called "Bridezillas." The show documented a number of engaged couples and followed them around in the months before their weddings.

What unfolded was mind-boggling: women manipulating, insulting, and getting down-right nasty with everyone involved with their wedding—all in the name of having "The Perfect Wedding." I cringed as I saw one bride tear apart her defenseless fiancé over the wedding invitations.

Of course, one doesn't have to be a so-called "Bridezilla" to be passionate about preparing for her wedding. The publishing world and the Internet alike provide soon-to-be brides with plenty of material to prepare for their dream day. Detailed timelines are included in every planner. For as far ahead as one year before the wedding, down to the last minute before the Bridal march, just about every waking second of every waking day is accounted for on these master timelines.

And the money. It is estimated that the average American wedding costs nearly $30,000 these days.[2] Where does all that money go? The flowers, the photographer, the church, the wedding gown, the reception hall, the videographer, the coordinator, the food, the guestbook, the favors, the musicians, gifts for the attendants—you name it, it has to be planned and paid for.

Thankfully, I was engaged for only about seven months before my wedding. I can't imagine being engaged for one or two years, as some people are. And thankfully too, my wonderful bride was anything but a Bridezilla. She was just the opposite. She would have preferred to have gone into a deep slumber for about six months and awakened on the morning of the wedding, surprised by how people had arranged her big day.

Yet, any good bride—and any father-of-the-bride who is worth his salt—knows that preparing for a wedding is essential. Without it, the grand and glorious "wedding of the century" cannot take place.

In short, without a prepared bride, there can be no wedding.

Tucked away in the heart of the book of Revelation, amidst the imagery of beasts and dragons and great harlots, sits a passage that unlocks all that we have been talking about thus far. And it too plays off the wedding imagery that we have just described.

The passage proclaims, "Let us be glad and rejoice and give [God] glory, for the marriage of the Lamb has come, and His wife has made herself ready" (Revelation 19:7). There it is—the marriage of the Lamb. A cause for great celebration indeed, as the "voice of a great multitude" (v. 6) extols. While earthly weddings are exciting in their own right, that glorious, cosmic wedding will be all the more so. Imagine being present at the "marriage of the Lamb." No Hollywood wedding, despite the millions they may cost, could even come close to the glory and splendor of that wonderful nuptial celebration.

Yet notice a very important element that this verse seems to play off. It ties in nicely with our current approach to weddings. What sets this glorious wedding day in motion? The voice of the great multitude proclaims, "For His wife has made herself ready." There it is: the key to understanding the long-delayed marriage of the Lamb! Through John the Revelator we are told that Christ's glorious wedding will take place when the bride has finally prepared herself.

The Greek word used here is "*hetoimazo*," which literally means to "prepare" or "make ready." We'll soon see the relevance of knowing this information.

Commenting on Revelation 19:7, Ranko Stefanovic notes,

> The preparation of the Lamb's bride . . . must be understood in the context of the ancient Hebrew wedding. The Hebrew wedding usually began with the betrothal at the house of the bride's father, where the groom paid the dowry. Afterwards, the two were considered husband and wife. The groom then returned to his father's house to prepare the place where he and his bride would live. During that time, the bride stayed at her father's home, preparing herself for the wedding. When both the place and the bride were ready, the bridegroom would return to take the bride to his father's house where the wedding ceremony was to take place.[3]

Does this imagery ring any bells—a groom paying a dowry and then returning to his father's house to prepare it for his bride, after which he returns to bring his bride back to his father's house? Does it ring a bell at all? I'm sure you're already three steps ahead of me.

This imagery should turn our attention to another book written by John the Revelator: the Gospel of John. In the 14th chapter we read the comforting words of Jesus to His disciples, "Let not your heart be troubled: you believe in God, believe also in Me." And then, as if he were speaking to a bunch of engaged Jewish men who could think of nothing else but getting married, He says, "In My Father's house are many mansions: if it were not so, I would have told you. I go to prepare a place for you."

The disciples, of course, knew exactly what Jesus was talking about. The Hebrew scriptures—what we call the "Old Testament"—were filled with imagery of God's marriage to His people. To the disciples, the wonderful news was that Jesus was about to fulfill His marital duties. And thus, He continues, "And if I go to prepare a place for you, I will come again and receive you to Myself; that where I am, there you may be also."

Jesus' words in this "oft' quoted" passage were nothing more than a picture of His marital intentions as reflected in the customs of His day: Man and woman are betrothed. Man returns to father's house to prepare it for his bride, while bride prepares herself. When both are prepared, they return to the father's house to get to "know" each other.

The ideas in John 14 and Revelation 19 complement one another. John, the author of both books, chooses the same Greek word to describe each scenario—*hetoimazo*. In John 14, Jesus proclaims, "I go to prepare [*hetoimazo*—to prepare, make ready] a place for you. And if I go to prepare [*hetoimazo*] a place for you, I will come again and receive you to Myself." The connecting word in each verse—*hetoimazo*—seems to lie at the center of the issue.

Thus, in our cosmic wedding checklist, there are two items that need to be addressed: first, the preparing of the Father's "mansions" in heaven and secondly, the preparing of the bride here on earth. Not until each has been prepared can a wedding take place.

This Hebrew wedding custom was recently illustrated to me in one of the churches I used to pastor. The daughter of two of my members was supposed to be getting married in the summer, and the rush was on. All of the wedding preparations were going full speed ahead, but surprisingly the wedding was moved up a few months. Instead of being in the summer, the wedding was actually rescheduled to the preceding March.

I had never heard of this before. Usually it's the other way around. If anything, the wedding is postponed a few months, sometimes even a year. The worst situation is when it's postponed indefinitely, which can't bode well for anyone—especially the father who's already shelled out nearly $30,000 for his daughter's "dream" wedding.

So why the hastened wedding day? Why the hurry? Apparently, the groom-to-be was building a house for his soon-to-be-wife and he had finished ahead of schedule. Needless to say, he was a little excited. Thus, the house was ready—it was prepared—why not have the wedding sooner?

That would be dependent, of course, on the bride's preparation as well. Imagine the young man's disappointment had the bride not been ready sooner. Fortunately, she too was prepared, and the wedding did take place months before its original date.

The parallels are tremendous. Here was a wedding that was actually hastened because of the young man's excitement. Yet, even if the young man had finished the house a year before, the wedding could only have taken place when the bride was ultimately ready.

When Jesus said that He was going to "prepare" a place for His bride, do you think He looked upon that task unexcitedly? Do you think He procrastinated when it came to it? Or do you think He, perhaps, was so excited about it that He couldn't wait to get the house finished for His bride?

How long would it take God to build a house, anyway? I suppose it depends on the size of it.

This line of reasoning is absurd, of course. It wouldn't take the God who built the entire world in six days a very long time to build a few houses, even if the houses are of the Bill Gates variety. (And why would we have any reason to believe that they're not?) It certainly wouldn't take Him 160 plus years to build these houses, let alone 2,000.

No, the same powerful Being who spoke the world into existence could finish His end of the wedding preparations in a matter of seconds. And not only that, He, like the young man who finished building the house for his fiancée sooner than anticipated, would be extremely excited to get the job done for His bride.

The truth is that Jesus has, indeed, finished His end of the wedding preparations. He's standing at the door, ready to return to earth and claim His bride. What's left then is for the bride's preparations to finally be completed, so the wedding can take place.

After all, that is what the "great multitude" was rejoicing about in Revelation 19:7. They weren't necessarily rejoicing because God had finished *His* preparations; they were rejoicing because His wedding was finally going to take place because "His wife has made herself ready." This is what will bring about that great and glorious wedding: the bride's being ready.

I'm sure a few of you feel uncomfortable with the implications just set forth. How can we, as finite human beings, have so much responsibility placed on our shoulders? We're nothing but sinful vessels who are poor representations of the God we serve and the beliefs we espouse.

Yet it is a very Biblical idea; God's bride (whom we will identify in the next chapter) has a huge part to play in how the Great Controversy unfolds. For some reason or another, God has chosen planet earth to be the battleground for His sparring match with Satan. In some senses, Shakespeare was right: "All the world's a stage and all the men and women merely players."

The apostle Peter certainly understood this truth when writing his second epistle. He wrote in 2 Peter 3:10, "But the day of the Lord will come like a thief. The heavens will disappear with a roar; the elements will be destroyed by fire, and the earth and everything in it will be laid bare." Thus, in light of Christ's soon coming, he admonished his readers, "Since everything will be destroyed in this way, what kind of people ought you to be? You ought to live holy and godly lives as you look forward to the day of God and speed its coming" (NIV).

Notice a few points that Peter brought forth. First, in light of the Second Coming, he encouraged his readers to "live holy and godly lives." This seems like a no-brainer to us, but Peter wanted to remind his audience of this important truth in the context of Christ's Second Coming. Of course, Peter expected his audience to live holy and godly lives all the time, but he especially wanted to remind them to live that way in light of Christ's Second Coming.

A few verses later, Peter somewhat repeated this admonition, but used stronger words, "So then, dear friends, since you are looking forward to this, make every effort to be found spotless, blameless and at peace with him" (v. 14, NIV).

Secondly, notice what Peter associated living a godly life with. He wrote, "You ought to live holy and godly lives as you look forward to the day of God and speed its coming." What a bold statement! Peter's implication is that Christ's people can actually speed up "the day of God." They can actually hasten (as many other versions translate this word) Christ's Second Coming.

And how is this accomplished? By living holy and godly lives—spotless and blameless. In other words: being prepared.

This preparation, of course, is not a preparation saturated in self-interest. The kind of preparation that I'm talking about is not discussed very often. In fact, when most people stress the idea of being "prepared" for Christ's coming, it's so that they can go to heaven with Him.

But this is not what the Bible means when talking about preparation. The Bible encourages God's people to be prepared so that Christ can come back in the first place. Nowhere does the Bible say, "Be ready when Christ returns so that you can go to heaven with Him." Instead, the Bible admonishes us, "Be ready *so that* Christ *can* return." Our preparedness enables Christ to come again.

Simply put, Christ can't get married without a bride. And He certainly can't return to earth if there isn't a group of people ready to meet Him.

I am fully aware that many of you are scared by these ideas, however. Some may even view them as being legalistic and some sort of "salvation by works" approach. But that couldn't be farther from the truth. Being prepared, in no way, ensures our salvation; no more than a bride being prepared for her wedding ensures that her husband will love her. The only thing that saves a person is the blood of Jesus. But that truth, when fully grasped, will be the igniting flame in the heart of the believer; that which prepares the bride in response to her loving Bridegroom.

Not long after my wife and I got married, my wife's brother Garrett and his girlfriend Jenny started talking about getting engaged. It was, of course, an exciting turn in their relationship, as it was for all of us who've traveled down that road. But it didn't come without a little anxiety.

You see, like any young lady, Jenny was eager about her big wedding day. She was very excited about the whole event and couldn't wait for it to take place. Actually, she was every bit as much excited about preparing for the wedding as she was excited about the day itself. Fortunately, Garrett and Jenny discussed marriage and had even decided on an approximate time that it would take place. The problem was, they still weren't officially engaged.

And Jenny began to get anxious, not because she was afraid they wouldn't get married, but because she wanted to make sure she would have enough time to prepare herself for the wedding. In fact, she would regularly remind Garrett of how many months she would need to get ready for the wedding, implying that he had better ask soon. She desperately wanted to scour the bridal magazines and look at wedding dresses, but she didn't dare do it before they were engaged.

But Garrett played it cool. He had something up his sleeve, and he wanted to pull off the perfect proposal. (You can ask him how he did it if you ever see him around.) He needed a little more time.

One night, a few days before Garrett was finally ready to propose, the two of them were saying their goodnights, and Jenny cutely whispered to Garrett, "Goodnight, Garrett; don't forget to ask me to marry you."

Talk about a young lady eager to get going on the wedding preparations! Yet what a wonderful picture of an eager bride, anxious to prepare for her wedding. And what a great reminder to all of us.

The beauty of the Gospel tells us that Christ did pay that dowry for us 2000 years ago on Calvary. He paid that dowry with His own blood. And then He did return to His Father's house to prepare a place for His bride.

But what about His bride? Has she, like Jenny and so many other brides, eagerly begun the wedding preparations? God has done His part; has she, by God's grace, done hers? Christ is waiting at the altar for such a thing to take place.

NOTES

1. http://www.cbsnews.com/stories/2002/08/20/earlyshow/leisure/books/main519238.shtml

2. http://money.cnn.com/2005/05/20/pf/weddings/?cnn=yes

3. Ranko Stefanovic, *Revelation of Jesus Christ* (Berrien Springs, Mich.: Andrews University Press, 2002), 541.

CHAPTER IV

THE "R" WORD

THE REMNANT.

What goes through your mind when you hear this word? I'm sure for many the thoughts aren't pleasant. Perhaps thoughts of anger, frustration, pain, hurt, or disappointment echo through the annals of your mind. As William G. Johnsson notes, "'Remnant' has become a four-letter word in some Adventist circles."[1]

Or maybe you are outraged at the idea that a group of people could consider themselves *The* Remnant. How can any one group of people claim that they are *The* Remnant, implying that all other groups are, therefore, mere pretenders? In this pluralistic, postmodern society, isn't there room for many churches? Don't all roads, in one way or another, lead to Rome?

And how is it that there are multiple groups claiming to be *The* Remnant? Seventh-day Adventists aren't the only ones who lay claim to this exclusive title. According to Jon Krakauer, in his book *Under the Banner of Heaven*, at any given moment there are 60,000 Mormon missionaries around the world who, along with their church leadership, "assert that the Church of Jesus Christ of Latter-day Saints [Mormonism] is mankind's 'one true church,' and that all other religions are false."[2]

Who's to say that the Mormon church, though owning one of the bloodiest histories among American religions, isn't the true Remnant? Who's to say that their religious beliefs aren't more in line with the truth than Seventh-day Adventists' beliefs? Or who's to say that Jehovah's Witnesses, Baptists, Catholics, or any other of the thousands of denominations aren't closer to the truth than we are? And more importantly, does it matter if a church has the "truth," but isn't loving?

Furthermore, as long as we all believe in Jesus Christ as our personal Savior, does it really matter which church holds our membership? Aren't we all going to the same place in the end, anyway?

Interestingly, according to a 1999 Gallup Poll, most Americans feel this way. When asked if they thought other religions, even those outside of Christianity, offered a true path to God, 75% of respondents replied in the affirmative. And of those 75% who responded in the affirmative, 82% felt that other religions were "equally as good" in being a pathway to God.[3] For them, more than one road seems to lead to heaven.

To be fair to biblical truth, however, we must reconcile these ideas with the text we looked at in the last chapter. As Revelation 19:7 proclaims, "Let us be glad and rejoice and give Him glory, for the marriage of the Lamb has come, and His wife has made herself ready." Who is that "wife" that Revelation talks about? To be sure, we plainly see that it says "wife" and not "wives," but what are the implications of this?

I'm sure you're tired of all the question marks that have found their way onto the first few pages of this chapter, and rightfully so. But in order to provide Christ with that bride that He longs to wed, we must grapple with these concepts. To do that, we must first identify the bride of Revelation 19.

A small caveat is first in order.

I have to admit that there was a time not too long ago when I was very turned off by the idea of a group calling itself "The Remnant." Though for my whole life I have been a part of a faith-community that has labeled itself this, I felt that it was a very elitist and self-congratulatory title. And rightfully so. I freely admit that many people within the walls of the Seventh-day Adventist church have this elitist attitude. I portray such a mindset far too often as well, I'm afraid.

But this reality should not scare us into throwing the baby out with the bathwater. Such an attitude stems from a fundamental misunderstanding of what it means to be the Remnant. Those of us who arrogantly boast that we are the Remnant probably aren't, in reality, truly a part of such a humble group. Rightfully so have many people within our own walls reacted negatively against such a hideous and horrendous idea.

The truth is, being a part of the Remnant doesn't give anyone brownie points. It doesn't mean that God loves members of such a group anymore than another group. It doesn't mean that at the heavenly potlucks such people can flash a membership card and go to the head of the line for first dibs on the Special K loaf.

Rather, being a part of the Remnant is less a reward and more of a responsibility. In fact, those who a part of such a group are in much greater danger of forfeiting eternal life than those who are outside this group. After all, Jesus poignantly declared, "For everyone to whom much is given, from him much will be required; and to whom much has been committed, of him they will ask the more" (Luke 12:48).

So before we start patting ourselves on the back, congratulating each other on a job well-done by being born or baptized into the Remnant, we need to take a long, hard look into the mirror and understand that God has placed an awesome responsibility on our shoulders rather than given us a ticket into heaven. When God chose Israel long ago, he keenly reminded them that it was not because they were bigger or better than any other nation. On the contrary, the Lord informed them that they "were the least of all peoples" (Deuteronomy 7:7) and that He only chose them because of His great love for them and the oath that He swore to their fathers. Such is a poignant reminder to us.

Nevertheless, the idea of there being a Remnant is a very biblical idea. And if we are going to humble ourselves under the authority of scripture, it is a concept that we must grapple with. Throughout the entire book of Revelation, this group keeps popping up its head, begging to be identified.

In Revelation 12:17, for example, we plainly read that the dragon "was enraged with the woman, and he went to make war with the rest of her offspring." The Greek word for "rest" here is *loipos*, and the *King James Version* actually translates this as "remnant." The word literally means "remaining," or that which is left over.

Elsewhere, in chapter 14 we read of the 144,000 who have a special relation to God. Although not employing the word *loipos* as before, this is, evidently, the same group of people that John refers to throughout his entire book. As with Revelation 12:17, he describes these people as they who "keep the commandments of God" (Revelation 14:12).

This also must be the same group of people that we read about it Revelation 19:7—the bride that finally makes herself ready for the wedding. This bride is also described in chapter 21 as the "New Jerusalem," which comes down out of heaven and takes its place on earth. While many of us read Revelation 21 as a description of what the heavenly city will look like—complete with its streets of gold and sea of glass—this chapter is actually describing what Christ's *bride* looks like.

After all, buildings and streets don't necessarily constitute a city—if anything, a place that has empty streets and vacant buildings would be called a "ghost town," not a city.

What really make a city are the people. Boston—the greatest city this side of the New Jerusalem, in my humble opinion—would not be considered a city if it just had tall buildings, nice houses, or winding, one-way streets (which are the cause of many frustrated drivers, I might add). What makes Boston a city is the fact that people live there.

It's the same with the New Jerusalem. What makes it a city, and thus worthy of Christ's hand in marriage, is the fact that people comprise it. Christ, after all, wouldn't wed a bunch of buildings.

Thus, perhaps—and I know this may sound scandalous— the portrayal of the New Jerusalem in Revelation 21 is actually describing the character of God's people, rather than simply giving us a Century 21 advertisement of what heaven looks like. (I am not saying that heaven isn't beautiful, though I wonder what it would do to our Christian aspirations if it weren't.)

So the evidence of Revelation is abundantly clear that there is a specific and identifiable group of individuals that constitute God's people. There are not 10 groups that make up this bride, but one, clear, distinguishable group that God has in these last days.

Yet I'm sure many people are still uneasy with this concept. After all, why is it necessary that there be only *one* group of individuals? And why is there a need for a Remnant at all? Such an attitude naturally produces elitism and an "us vs. them" mentality. This has been evidenced throughout the history of the world. One need not look any further than the front page of a newspaper to see that this is still abundantly prevalent today. Never mind the Crusades or the Holocaust of centuries gone by; such prejudiced attitudes in the name of religion exist today in places like Northern Ireland, Sudan, and the Middle East. When a person supposes that his religion trumps all other religions, such hatred and animosity naturally arises in the human heart.

I would remind you, however, that the Remnant naturally has no such animosity. By definition, God's Remnant people understand their awesome responsibility to love, rather than to be arrogantly exclusive and filled with hate.

At the same time, those individuals who are a part of God's Remnant also recognize that God has His people in all walks of life. Rightfully so do many critics of a Remnant concept quote John 10:16. There we read Jesus' words: "And other sheep I have which are not of this fold." While Jesus was referring to Israel of His day as the "fold," we can easily apply this to the religious landscape of today. God has His people in all faiths.

Interestingly, Adventism's own prophet poignantly declared in 1888 that "the greater part of the followers of Christ" are "without doubt, in the various churches professing the Protestant faith."[4] This would be scandalous to us if we did not recognize that there are many sincere and devoted followers of Christ—who are living up to the light they have been given—in every religious body. One need not be a card-carrying member of the Adventist church to be under the caring shepherding of Christ.

Yet too many people stop reading John 10:16 after the first sentence, failing to see the significance of the rest of the verse. After declaring that He has sheep in other folds, Jesus went on to say, "Them also I must bring, and they will hear My voice and there will be one flock and one shepherd." The purpose of the Remnant is to be a united collection of all God's sheep. Rather than having sheep scattered throughout various folds, Christ's ultimate goal in these last days is to bring all his sheep into one flock.

This one flock that Christ longs to have is not for the purpose of being a social club, complete with blonde-haired and blue-eyed elites. Christ's Remnant is a group that He can point to and say, "This is My bride. This is the group of individuals that most closely reflect My character of love."

The idea of a Remnant is nothing more than a by-product of God's amazing mercy and grace. Rather than keep searching and hurting souls in the dark, Christ, in His mercy, has appointed a special group of people who are the responsible agents of His love—a group that other people can align themselves with to enjoy love, fellowship, and a deepening understanding of God. One need not search aimlessly throughout his or her whole life to try to find such a group. God's Word makes the distinguishing marks of this Remnant abundantly clear.

Amazingly, the Seventh-day Adventist church matches up most closely with the distinguishing marks of Revelation—and, indeed, the rest of Scripture. Not only is the Seventh-day Adventist church one of the only churches that champions all 10 of the commandments God gave at Mt. Sinai, but it uplifts the faith and testimony of Jesus Christ—the latter also known as the "spirit of prophecy" (Revelation 19:10).

Clifford Goldstein, himself a former atheist who joined the Adventist church later in life, wrote, "No other corporate body approaches the present truth that

Adventism has." He added, "If a seeker for truth can find a church that fits the prophecies concerning the remnant better than Adventism does . . . then that person ought to join such a church."[5]

This is not to say that the Seventh-day Adventist church is perfect. It is not to say that other denominations do not have certain elements of the truth as well. Nor is this to deny the fact that many people have been deeply hurt by the Adventist church or individuals who belong to it.

It is to say, however, that the Seventh-day Adventist church most closely matches the characteristics that the book of Revelation attributes to Christ's bride. And more than simply producing a group of people that sits back and feels satisfied with the status quo, this group naturally feels the awesome responsibility to deepen its understanding of truth and lovingly uplift the matchless charms of its Savior to a dying and hurting world. Rather than feeling good and smug about their status, these people feel the need to accurately portray the love of the Groom.

As I was thinking about a way to close this chapter, I wanted to find a compelling story to illustrate the importance of identifying the Remnant and the awesome responsibility that goes along with such a title. I was initially perplexed.

And then I thought of my brother-in-law, Cameron. After spending four demanding and grueling years at Loma Linda University, he recently graduated from medical school. He's now officially a doctor, doing his residency in Chattanooga, Tennessee. He hopes to ultimately go into sports medicine.

As a doctor in the United States, Cameron is part of a pretty exclusive group of individuals. Although the reputation of medical doctors has, unfortunately, been on the decline a bit in recent years—as is evidenced by the constant presence of medical malpractice cases—society still esteems doctors very highly. We still admire their commitment, dedication, and tremendous ability to care for the health and well-being of society-at-large.

Many doctors are a part of the American Medical Association, a group of doctors that are committed to the advancement of medicine. Their mission is "to promote the art and science of medicine and the betterment of public health."[6]

It just so happens that members of the American Medical Association also enjoy a higher salary than a lot of other professions. It's no secret that doctors make a few more shekels than a lot of other people—especially those of us in the pastoral ministry.

Thus, we could look at the American Medical Association and be very critical of it. We could sit back and criticize members of this group because they arrogantly drive around BMWs and live in multi-million dollar mansions, as their bank accounts multiply by the thousands. We could say that being a part of such a group naturally produces an elitist attitude.

Or, we could be thankful that such a group has been formed and identified, thus allowing us to know who is responsible for saving lives in this country. We need not be in the dark anymore as to who we can turn to when we have a medical problem. Because this association has been established, we know where we can find help in times of need. We know the group of individuals that is constantly working for the "betterment of public health."

And so it is with the Remnant. If no such group were formed or identified, who would step forward and take responsibility for doing God's last-day work? Everyone would be exonerated of responsibility. No bride would approach the altar, taking Christ's hand in marriage.

Furthermore, if no such group were formed and identified, the world would be at a loss as to where they could turn to understand Christ's saving love. While other churches outside of Adventism try to portray this responsibility of love, their understanding falls fundamentally short on many levels.

Some may object that the Adventist church falls infinitely short of truly fulfilling its responsibility to uplift Christ's unconditional love. This, I have no argument against. I do not deny such an idea. But that is the precise reason why this book is being written.

NOTES

1. William G. Johnsson, "In Defense of the Remnant," *Adventist Review*, May 14 (1998), 5.

2. Jon Krakauer, *Under the Banner of Heaven* (New York: Anchor Books, 2004), 364.

3. 1999 Gallup Poll (Wilmington, Del.: Scholarly Resources, Inc.), 281, 282.

4. Ellen G. White, *The Great Controversy* (Mountain View, Calif.: Pacific Press Publishing Association, 1907), 383.

5. Clifford Goldstein, *The Remnant* (Boise, Idaho: Pacific Press Publishing Association, 1994), 92.

6. http://www.ama-assn.org/ama/pub/category/1815.html. Accessed on August 16, 2007.

CHAPTER V

THE KNOCKING

One of my college professors warned all of his students to never read the book Song of Solomon unless we were married. We wondered if he was joking, but we soon realized that he was being serious. It seemed kind of odd for a religion professor to tell his students not to read a part of the Bible, but it takes little reflection to realize the validity of his concern.

To say the least, the Song of Solomon is provocative. It's not the kind of stuff you'd want your eight-year-old son to pick up and read, though my father, a pastor, once encouraged this during a sermon one Sabbath when I was very young. I went home and read it, of course. And I wasn't even married yet. I was scandalized.

Amid the romantic interplay between the main characters in the book, the two expound upon curvaceous thighs, breasts that are like the clusters of a palm tree, and many other sexual innuendos and euphemisms that many commentators see elsewhere in the book. Who needs Danielle Steele or *Desperate Housewives* when they can read the Song of Solomon?

And thus, the book has puzzled commentators and lay persons for generations. They are baffled as to the meaning and reason behind this book. Many liberal scholars, who don't necessarily hold to a strict belief in the Holy Spirit's influence in forming the canon of Scripture, wonder whether it should really be in the Bible at all. Those who are of the more conservative persuasion and believe that all 66 books in the Bible belong there are equally baffled by its placement too, however. In the end, they are left scratching their head as to its meaning.

Many explanations are given regarding this controversial book. Some see it as allegorical, showing a picture of the love-relationship between God and His people—whether that was Israel of old or His church today. Others feel as though it is simply a book that portrays the relationship between two individuals who are madly in love, speaking nothing of the relationship between God and His people. Still, others see in the Song of Solomon a kind of Christian "sex manual," if you will, for those who want to follow God in this important area of life.

One thing is for sure, however: the Song of Solomon, which is also known as the Song of Songs, isn't going away any time soon. Long before Christ was born, long before the apostle Paul wrote his "Love Chapter" in 1 Corinthians 13, the Song of Solomon was set aside to be a part of the Hebrew Bible (and thus, a part of our Holy Bible today). Christ, no doubt, read from it when He walked this earth—maybe even in His childhood. Why shouldn't we do the same? It was Paul, after all, who wrote, "All scripture is God-breathed and is useful for teaching, rebuking, correcting, and training in righteousness" (2 Timothy 3:16, NIV). He was speaking directly of the Old Testament, which included the Song of Solomon (even in his day).

Interestingly, one of the most pleasant descriptions of this book came from the pen of a Jewish rabbi who lived a few short years after Christ. "Heaven forbid that any man in Israel ever disputed that the Song of Songs is holy," wrote Rabbi Aqiba, "For the whole world is not worthy of the day on which the Song of Songs was given to Israel." He then concluded, "All the Writings are holy [but] the Song of Songs is the Holy of Holies."[1]

Song of Solomon: The Holy of Holies. I like that. And perhaps he's on to something. As Christ ministers in the Most Holy Place—the "Holy of Holies" in heaven—and tries to wed His bride, perhaps we find a grand picture of this truth in the book that Aqiba titles the same. Because, even though I believe this book has many literal qualities to it and can enlighten our minds in the area of sexuality, I believe the Holy Spirit directed its placement in Scripture to reveal a grander truth of God's character. As Jesus declared, "These are they which testify of Me" (John 5:39). He was referring to the whole of Scripture, which includes the Song of Solomon.

Thus, in the end, the Song of Solomon shares a true picture of Christ for His people. As one person described this book, it is "The Love-Life of the Lord."[2] It portrays a love-affair between God and His bride-to-be. There is much to be learned from this wonderful book, then, in the context of our pursuits.

The Song of Solomon shares a picture of a young Shulamite woman who has been swept off her feet by her "beloved." Though some would say the book doesn't necessarily share a chronological story between the two lovers, it does definitely show a picture of two people who are madly in love. Amid all the lovely "sweet-nothings" that the two share with one another, however, something strange takes place in chapter five. It has perplexed commentators for ages.

Although the Shulamite is definitely smitten with her "Casanova," chapter five relates an unfortunate and perplexing event. Half-asleep and dreaming, the young lady hears a knocking on her bedroom door. "I sleep, but my heart is awake," she says, "it is the voice of my beloved! He knocks, saying, 'Open for me, my sister, my love, my dove, my perfect one; for my head is covered with dew, my locks with the drops of the night'" (Song of Solomon 5:2).

This is no ordinary knocking, however. The Hebrew word used for "knock" gives the impression of a downright beating of the door. The Shulamite's lover wants to make sure that he awakens his lover, and he is eager to have her open the door.

I can remember a few experiences that I've had in knocking on doors, though not on my lover's. I'm ashamed to admit the circumstances, but it was when I was helping with an evangelistic series and we went door-to-door knocking. I was often scared to have people actually answer the door and open it, so I would knock ever-so-lightly. It definitely wasn't a beating. Many times I would softly knock initially, wait a few seconds, and then knock softly again. If no one answered after the second attempt, I would be on my merry way, relieved that I didn't have to actually speak with someone.

This is not the attitude of the "beloved," however. He wants entry. He wants the Shulamite to wake up and open the door. Thus, there is no light knocking coming from his hand. There is a beating.

To be sure, the Shulamite definitely hears the knocking, and her heart skips a beat when she hears the voice of her beloved. What more could a young lady want than to have her lover come knocking on her door late at night?

But surprisingly, she has a startling response. Almost annoyed with being awakened in the middle of the night, she says, "I have taken off my robe; how can I put it on again? I have washed my feet; how can I defile them?" (v. 3). In other words, "Come back another time when it's more convenient for me."

What a response to a man she supposedly loves and is smitten with. It reminds me of when I finally did talk with Camille about pursuing a relationship, when I came "knocking" on her door. Though she was clearly "smitten" with me, she was very cautious about getting into a relationship. In fact, when I told my mother about her hesitancy, she began to cry because she thought that if Camille wasn't interested in pursuing a relationship, no one would ever want to date her son.

Camille, of course, ultimately did respond to my "knocking," and we started dating. But when the young Shulamite finally does decide to get up and open the door for her "beloved," it is too late, and he is nowhere to be found. When she goes out to look for him, the watchmen of the city find her and beat her up. It's not a glorious account of a woman who is allegedly in love and twinkle-eyed.

And this is precisely the Remnant's problem. Though allegedly "in love" and "smitten" with the Almighty, the Remnant refuse to open the door to Him. As He stands on our doorstep and knocks, asking us to open to Him, we slumber and sleep, groggy from the late night we had before. As Ellen F. Davis noted, "God makes an advance toward us when we do not expect it, seeking admittance to our hearts. But so often we are unwilling to lose any sleep or get our feet dirty when God approaches."[3]

Quite frankly, we don't want to be inconvenienced. We're happy with the status-quo. Like a young, twinkle-eyed girl, many of us would rather dream about our wedding day than actually participate in it or put forth the effort to prepare for it. In the same way, many of us would rather dream about heaven than actually participate in what heaven is truly all about. It's not a glorious description of a church that prides itself on being called the Remnant. And yet it's a truthful and real description.

But still God knocks. And He's not just *knocking* on our doors; He's beating on them, trying to get our attention. It's not that He's mad or upset; it's that He's serious about getting our attention, so He's doing all He can to draw a response from us. But it's almost as if the knocking is falling on deaf ears.

Incidentally, this is the same problem that faces the church of Laodicea in the book of Revelation. Though allegedly in love with the Lord, Christ approaches the church and says, "I know your works, that you are neither cold nor hot...So then, because you are lukewarm, and neither cold nor hot, I will vomit you out of My mouth" (Revelation 3:15, 17). So at the end of His message to the Laodiceans, He announces, "Behold, I stand at the door and knock. If anyone hears My voice and opens the door, I will come in to him and dine with him, and he with Me" (v. 20). Just as the "Beloved" in the Song of Solomon came knocking on the Shulamite's door, so too Christ comes knocking on Laodicea's door.

At first glance, the parallels may look incidental, but a closer look reveals a stronger connection. Whereas the English version, and even the original Hebrew text itself, doesn't convey the parallel, a look at the Greek version of the Song of Solomon reveals an interesting correlation. The Greek translation of the Old Testament (which the New Testament authors often quoted from instead of the Hebrew) quotes the Song of Solomon as saying, "I sleep, but my heart is awake: the voice of my kinsman knocks at the door" (LXE).

The Hebrew version doesn't include the words "at the door," but the Greek translation adds them. Similarly, Revelation 3:20 uses the exact same Greek words when relaying Christ's actions towards the church of Laodicea; Christ announces that He stands "at the door" and knocks.

Indeed, just as He wants His bride to open the door in the Song of Solomon, He wants His bride—the Laodicean church—to open the door to Him in Revelation. And sadly, just as His bride delays in opening the door in the Song of Solomon, it's apparent that His bride delays in opening the door to Him now.

It's interesting to note that in Christ's message to the Laodicean church, He addresses both the corporate church and the individual person. Not only does He speak to the church as a whole, but in verse 20 He proclaims, "Behold, I stand at the door and knock. If any*one* hears My voice... "

This tells us that Christ views the problem as being both a corporate and an individual dilemma. Indeed, He's knocking on the hearts of the church, His bride, as a whole, but He appeals to the individual as well. As many commentators note, this tells us that He desires an intimate heart-experience with each individual person that comprises the corporate bride. In other words, it starts with us as individuals.

The scene reminds me all too vividly of a picture of Jesus that used to hang on the walls of my room, which my brother and I shared growing up. It was hanging there until my brother decided it was time the room needed an "extreme makeover." Though I couldn't really lay claim to the room anymore, since I moved out and am now married, I returned home one day to find the whole room was totally different. The walls were bright blue; every thing that belonged to me was boxed up and in the attic; and the bed that I had slept in for 23 years was nowhere to be found. My personhood in that house had been mysteriously raptured.

Needless to say, it didn't breed feelings of goodwill. To be honest, I felt like a man without a home, one whose identity had been erased from the house I had called home for all but two years of my life. (To be fair, there were still other, smaller pictures of me hanging in various other parts of the house that at least gave some clue as to my presence in that house at one point in time.)

The picture of Jesus wasn't there, either. I guess it didn't go with the new "hot" blue color of the walls that my brother was going for. But although the picture had vanished, the scene it portrayed still resonates in my mind. Perhaps you've seen the picture too or a variation of it.

It shows Jesus standing at a door and knocking. And if you look with an observant eye, you'll notice that the door doesn't have a knob on the outside, a sure message that the only way the door will open is if its owner does so from within.

The message is unmistakable: Jesus will not force His way into our hearts. Yet the beauty of the Gospel tells us that He is definitely knocking. And, although the Song of Solomon portrays a Savior that "beats" on the door out of a sense of dire emergency, He is ever patient and tenderhearted in His appeals to win us over.

One of my seminary classmates, although not necessarily addressing this subject, profoundly observed in one of my classes recently, "Motivating people from a sense of responsibility doesn't work." In other words, merely informing Christ's bride that she is responsible for hastening the marriage of the Lamb isn't enough. Convicting people of the facts—that we have a part to play in this grand and climactic event—won't truly prepare the bride for the wedding either.

Only when Christ's bride, both the individual members and the collective body, truly opens the door to her Savior and has an intimate heart-experience with Him, can she truly prepare herself. Only when our hearts are melted with the realities of the Gospel and we respond to the One who gave His life for us, can we move on into a marital bliss with Him. And the reality is, in order for us to open the door to our Savior, we must first see a picture of Him that we've never seen before, a picture of the Groom that we cannot resist.

Even the Shulamite—that unfortunate woman who spurned her lover—had flattering things to say about her beloved. Just a few verses after she refuses to open the door to him, she longingly describes him as being "the chiefest among ten thousand" and one who is "altogether lovely" (Song of Solomon 5:10, 16).

To be sure, these words describe our Beloved as well. They describe the Man who knocks so urgently upon our doors. Will we allow ourselves to open the door and see His loveliness?

I recently read an unfortunate nuptial account that has happened more than once, I'm sure. It's a story of a wedding that had its attendees on the edge of their seats with nervousness, as well as 99% of its participants.

As the story goes, everything was all set for this wedding to take place. The guests were all seated; the minister was ready to join the two young people in holy matrimony; the organist was playing the preliminary music; the groom was even in his place. But something wasn't right. When the clock struck 12, so to speak, and it was time for the wedding, it delayed. Five minutes passed. Ten minutes passed. Fifteen minutes passed. And still, the wedding lingered.

At this point, as you can imagine, the guests in the audience started quietly stirring. They began looking at one another, wondering why the wedding hadn't yet begun. Then, everyone started looking towards the back of the church, curious to see why the bride wasn't yet marching down the aisle. Not surprisingly, the hopeful groom felt the same sense of nervousness that the crowd did. He also focused his eyes on the back of the church, but the only thing he saw was the wedding coordinator frantically running around the foyer of the church.

You see, the bride was nowhere to be found.

Of all the things that could happen on the day of the wedding, perhaps this was the most surprising and alarming. What happened to the bride? Did she have second thoughts? Was it another case of a "Runaway Bride"?

Realizing that the bride was missing, some of the bridal party retreated from their positions in the church and started looking for her as well. Some ran outside, yelling her name. Others searched high and low in the balcony or in the basement. She was nowhere to be found.

And then they heard a most curious sound coming from a small room in the basement of the church. A very distinct, familiar sound.

Knocking. Banging. Yelling. Screaming.

They quickly ran over to the room where the noise was coming from, realizing that the bride had locked herself in the room and was furiously knocking on its door to have someone let her out. Here was a bride, late to her own wedding because she couldn't open the door.

It seems to me that Christ's bride has the same problem. The marriage of the Lamb has been delayed because His bride has locked herself in and won't open the door. This time, however, it's not that she *can't* open the door, it's that she *won't*.

Are we going to finally open the door to Christ? After all, is it a foregone conclusion that, in the end, God gets the girl? It hasn't happened yet. To be sure, we see clear Biblical evidence that He must. But God can't really "get the girl" until that girl wants to be gotten, until she stops playing hard-to-get.

The beauty of the Gospel tells us that Christ will keep knocking until He gets our attention. But let's not make it harder than it has to be. Let's submit ourselves to the One who is "altogether lovely" and is truly worthy of our utmost love and admiration.

I love Jesus' words in Luke 12:36. They have great relevance to us today. "Be like men waiting for their master to return from a wedding banquet, so that when he comes and knocks they can immediately open the door for him" (NIV).

He's knocking. In all His loveliness. The most handsome Groom that ever was is longingly knocking on our door. Will we open to Him?

NOTES

1. Mishnah Yadayim 3:5
2. A. B. Simpson, *The Love-Life of the Lord* (New York: Christian Alliance Publishing Co).
3. Ellen F. Davis, *Proverbs, Ecclesiastes, and the Song of Songs* (Louisville: Westminster John Knox Press, 2000), 277.

SECTION TWO

THE WAITING GROOM

CHAPTER VI

Anywhere, Vt. – You never know what you'll see on the back roads of Vermont. It's the reason that people literally come from thousands of miles away to venture down these roads paved with dirt; they want to experience life in the slow lane. Yet, while most people flock to Vermont's byways to witness the best fall foliage the world has to offer, or to enjoy the scenes of a quaint, little town—complete with a white church and country store—what I saw one particular winter afternoon surpasses anything I'm sure anyone would ever expect to see.

There, in the back woods of Vermont, in the Middle-of-Nowhere, I saw men in orange. Have you ever seen men in orange? In Vermont? I suppose the only men in orange you have ever seen were prison inmates who were on work assignment along the highway; but these were not convicts. Not only were they wearing orange, but they also had hairless heads.

I couldn't believe my eyes when I drove by them. In the dead of winter they were walking around outside, barely draped in these orange robes. They were Buddhist monks.

Of course, I naturally thought that something was wrong. Perhaps my eyes had mistaken me or I was driving too fast. But sure enough, when I reached my destination a few minutes later and asked my hosts about it, they confirmed that these were indeed Buddhist monks. In fact, some of the people's children had worked for the monks, mowing their lawns and cleaning up their compound.

Amazingly, this type of scene isn't rare in Vermont. Apparently there are dozens of these Buddhist communities that line the tiny state. One website I visited declared that, per capita, Vermont has the most "Caucasian Buddhists" in the United States. Actually, when one reflects upon the varied climate of Vermont's inhabitants, it shouldn't come as a surprise. (During the last elections, I had the opportunity to vote for someone from the "Marijuana Party" to be governor. I kindly declined the offer.)

But that encounter spurred my interest in Buddhism. Not to the point of converting, as one of my friends joked with me when he noticed I was reading about the eastern religion; but out of curiosity. That, and the fact that a person directed my attention toward Buddhism's founder—Siddhartha Gotama—after I preached a sermon on the incarnation of Christ.

Surprisingly, you may have more in common with your Buddhist neighbor than you first thought.

I'm sure that many of you are quite alarmed with the first few paragraphs of this chapter. After explaining to you a few chapters ago that the Seventh-day Adventist church is God's true Remnant church—His bride—on earth, am I now going to try to convert you to Buddhism? That is not the case at all.

As I said, the reason I am writing about Buddhism is because of a few similarities between it and Christianity that were brought to my attention. One Sabbath, as I preached a Christmas sermon on the incarnation of Christ, I announced to the audience that I had not found anyone throughout the history of the world who had thrown aside his or her royal and financial superiority to live with his or her subjects. I did a Google search to try to find someone—anyone—who fit this description. But no one turned up.

To my knowledge (and Google's too), there was not one person in earth's history that did what God did by living among His people. No prince, king, or president decided that he would throw aside his high status and riches and live among the paupers. Sure, there have been people like Mother Theresa or Francis of Assisi, but they weren't exactly royalty before they did such a thing.

But after the sermon, as people were walking out of the sanctuary and I was greeting them, two individuals were called to my attention by two astute gentlemen. The first one was Michael Dukakis. If you've never heard of him, you are either too young or you are not from Massachusetts.

He was the much-beleaguered Governor of Massachusetts that ran for president against the elder George Bush in 1988. He lost in a landslide vote, winning only ten states. The "Duke," as he was called, just didn't steal the hearts of Americans, or even many people from his home state.

Perhaps the only thing that made him stand out, according to my friend at church who pointed this out to me, was that he would actually take a public bus to work every day from his home in Brookline, Massachusetts. He would literally ride among the "common folk" as he commuted to the state house in Boston.

As you can see, the comparison is quite a stretch. Though he would suffer through the bus ride with the commoners, the good ol' Duke was returning home to luxury every day. Surely anyone can put up with "poverty" for a few hours each day, especially when he or she knows that paradise is on the other end of that journey.

The second person that was brought to my attention was Siddhartha Gotama, the person commonly attributed as being the founder of Buddhism. Apparently, according to the gentleman who pointed it out to me, the first Buddha left the affluent family that he was born into so he could experience a life of denial and poverty. That, of course, piqued my interest in finding out more about him.

Although there is some debate as to the details of Gotama's life and whether he truly was the first Buddha, historians pretty much agree that he came from a wealthy family. He was, in fact, known as a prince. But this position and status didn't bring true meaning and satisfaction, and he finally denied these luxuries to pursue a life of poverty. He was searching for the true meaning of life.

After six years of searching, he finally found it. He was sitting under a tree in Bodh Gaya, India, when the proverbial light dawned on him. Soon thereafter he formulated a group to follow him and his ideas, and the rest, as they say, is history.

With all due respect, however, Michael Dukakis and the Buddha fall infinitely short of God's great descent. As we noted, the Duke forfeited his luxuries for only a few hours a day, while the Buddha denied his wealth for his own benefit—he was searching for personal meaning. But what God did by becoming a man is unprecedented. It's not something that many people, whether rich or poor, strive for. While we, as humans, seek to climb higher, God's character is one that looks to lower itself.

Of course, the incarnation of Christ isn't the only place in scripture that this is seen.

Buddha isn't the only person to have a revelation while sitting under a tree. The Bible shows the picture of a God who also frequently liked to do the same. But while Buddha, a mere man, sat under a tree so he could search for something higher, God sat under a tree to reveal that that something Higher was searching for man.

The first place we see this illustrated is in the book of Genesis. We are told that during the "heat of day" the Lord "appeared" to Abraham by "the terebinth trees in Mamre" (Genesis 18:1). Being a good host, Abraham invited the Lord, along with His two companions, to rest under a tree while he retrieved water to wash their feet. It is, after all, a very hot day in the Middle East. Who wants to be standing in a place where there is no shade?

The second place we read about God revealing Himself under a tree is in the book of Judges. There, we read, "...the Angel of the Lord came and sat under the terebinth tree which was in Ophrah...and the Angel of the Lord appeared to [Gideon], and said to him, 'The Lord is with you, you mighty man of valor'" (Judges 6:11, 12). Unmistakably, the "Angel of the Lord" is Christ, Himself. After all, He declares to Gideon, "The Lord is with you."

It's amazing when you stop and think about it: God, sitting under a tree.

Yet the truth is, long before the nativity scene in Bethlehem, our Savior walked this earth and sat under the trees that He made with His own hands. It tells you a lot about His character. It tells you that He couldn't stand being apart from His created beings. And when an opportunity arose for a message to be sent from God to humanity, Christ eagerly and excitedly chose to deliver the message Himself. He wanted every excuse He could find to visit His loved ones and be among them.

What may come as a surprise to you is the fact that the whole Bible bears witness to this idea. God couldn't stand being separated from His creatures. From the very beginning God communed with Adam and Eve face-to-face in the Garden. And as soon as they sinned and severed that connection with Him, we still find a God eager to be with His people. Genesis 3:8 records that Adam and Eve "heard the sound of the Lord God walking in the garden." He was, no doubt, walking under the trees.

This idea especially finds root in the beautiful declaration that God made in Exodus 25:8. Through Moses, God tells the Children of Israel, "And let them make Me a sanctuary, that I may dwell among them."

In my opinion, this is one of the most beautiful passages in the whole Old Testament, if not the whole Bible. As I mentioned before, I've yet to find a royal being, either a human or a god, who desired to live among his people. Yet this is what God declares. He wants to live in the very presence of His people. He wants to be in their midst.

And it's not as if He wants to live on the outskirts of town surrounded by a thick forest and electric fences. My wife and I recently visited my father-in-law in North Carolina and we were interested in touring the Biltmore Estate, the country's largest privately owned home in Asheville. But it cost nearly thirty dollars each, and we quickly lost interest. The funny thing is, we couldn't even *see* the estate. The whole home, though within the limits of a fairly big city, is surrounded by hundreds of acres of forest, and you have to go through a gate to even get near the property.

God tells Moses to have His house built in the *middle* of the camp. It was smack-dab in the midst of the Children of Israel. He doesn't want to be an outside observer; He wants to be at the center of all that's going on.

It really is a mystery. Beneath a tree or in a tent, God wants nothing more than to be with His people. He will go to any length to restore the relationship that was lost when sin entered the world.

The idea of God camping among His people is echoed in the Gospel of John. We read in John 1:14, "And the Word became flesh and dwelt among us." I love how Eugene Peterson, in *The Message*, translates this. He writes, "The Word became flesh and blood, and moved into the neighborhood." Yet the original Greek shares even more insight into this amazing idea. The Greek actually says that the Word became flesh and "tabernacled" or "tented" among us, a sure fulfillment of what the Old Testament sanctuary pointed to.

It's kind of a neat thought, if you ask me. As a person who has enjoyed many camp meetings, I can picture God taking up residence in one of those bland green or orange army tents. I've yet to see, by the way, a conference president who has actually camped out at a camp meeting. They usually do the Michael Dukakis thing and return home to their luxurious palaces at the end of the day (and I don't blame them!).

One of my worst nights of camping came when I, along with my brother and cousins, decided to camp in Key West, Florida during spring break one particular year. For some reason, we thought it would be a great idea. (For those of you who aren't familiar with Key West, it's not exactly known for its righteous living, especially during college spring break time.) We failed to realize that every college-age student in the United States would be camping at our campground, partying until sunrise.

We were surrounded by young people who were drinking, dancing, smoking all kinds of things, and engaging in other unmentionable activities. In all honesty, and I don't wish to offend anyone from Key West when I say this: I felt as if I were camping in the middle of Sodom and Gomorrah. I didn't really sleep that night. I absolutely cringed at what was going on around me, and I felt out of place. Of course, if I had been truly Christ-like, I would have come out of my shelter and mingled with the other people instead of hiding in a tent of self-righteousness.

But this is the mystery of the incarnation. So great is God's love and His desire to be with His people that He left

His heavenly home to live among His creatures. Indeed, so great is His love that He camped among them. Whereas I hid myself in my tent while camping in Key West, Christ fully submersed Himself in the affairs of his people. He didn't just live among the people as a recluse; He was involved with their everyday experiences.

Though a holy God, He surrounded Himself with things that were so contrary to who He was. Though perfectly pure, Christ lived among the impure. Though perfectly holy, He lived among the unholy. Though perfectly loving, He lived among the unloving. Every part of His being should have revolted against that which surrounded Him.

Yet so great was God's love for this lost world that He couldn't help but incarnating Himself as a human being. And it's not as though God was taking a break from His normal character and actions. Paul, while writing to the church in Philippi, said, "Let this mind be in you which was also in Christ Jesus, who, being in the form of God, did not consider it robbery to be equal with God, but made Himself of no reputation, taking the form of a bondservant, and coming in the likeness of men" (Philippians 2:5-7).

Most people interpret this to mean that Christ, although He was God, didn't consider it to be an esteemed position. In other words, even though Christ was God, He didn't really envy the role. Yet, as Gerald F. Hawthorne points out in his commentary, one could actually translate this passage, "Christ Jesus, who—*precisely because he was in very nature God*—did not consider equality with God to be ground for grasping..." While the first way of interpretation implies that Christ's incarnation was contrary to His character, the second implies that it was the reason for it.[1]

C.F.D. Moule further illustrates this by noting that most people view the incarnation as a "V-pattern of descent followed by ascent." However, God views the incarnation, not as a "V-pattern," but as "a straight line of equation."[2] The incarnation, far from being a step-down in God's eyes, was the crowning achievement in His revelation of love.

To our feeble human minds, we can't understand how God could become a man. We don't understand how the most powerful Being in the whole universe could become a human fetus in the womb of a teenage girl for nine months and then be born a crying and naked baby. In our minds, that goes against everything we know to be normal and admirable. Yet that's who God is. In all His beauty.

The story of God's incarnation reminds me all too vividly of an experience I had in my early days of ministry. I told one of my church members, whose father was no longer a member of the church, that I wanted to come by and visit with her. She was all too excited to host me. But I was conflicted about visiting with her—mostly because she lived so far away.

But I finally decided to go. I trekked the 90 minutes to her town and pulled into the driveway, noticing one of the sorriest looking trailer homes I had ever seen. As I parked the car in the driveway, she came running out to greet me, excited about being honored with her pastor's presence. Entering the house, I couldn't believe my eyes. I kid you not; it was one of the dirtiest homes I have ever been in. There were dirty clothes flung across the floor, magazines stacked nearly to the roof, dishes piled up in the sink, and just a foul air about the place. Though I've never been accused of being the cleanest person in the world (just ask my wife), every part of me shuddered by being in the midst of the filth.

Incidentally, her father was there. He was very nice and cordial towards me. But the whole time I was there visiting with the two of them, I stood in the middle of the living room. They didn't even invite me to sit down, probably because there was nowhere to sit. It was a very odd experience. The funniest part of the whole visit, however, came when the father said, "It's a good thing you don't look at my daughter's room. It's so dirty."

In my mind, however, I couldn't get out of there fast enough. Yet in our conversation, I came to a deep realization about their situation. In that conversation it was revealed to me that this young lady's mother had hanged herself a few years before and that her younger sister was estranged from them, living in Missouri. Her father also did all he could to support the two of them by working all day. To say the least, the girl had a sad situation.*

As I drove home after the visit, an insurmountable wave of guilt came rushing over me. I felt guilty because my family situation was so much better than hers and because I felt disgusted by being in their filthy house. I also felt guilty because I hadn't wanted to go there in the first place. I said to myself over and over, "Shame on me. Shame on me. Shame on me."

It also helped me realize, on a much smaller scale, just how much of a sacrifice God made by becoming a Man. I couldn't stand to be surrounded by filth for 30 minutes, yet Christ lived on this earth for over 30 years, surrounded by far greater filth and dirt than I have ever experienced. And as I reflected upon God's great descent in the light of my short visit, my heart became incredibly overwhelmed with God's infinite love. A love that surpasses anything I could ever hope to imagine or imitate.

It's amazing when you stop and think about it. After all, what good is a Groom who won't reach down to His bride's level, or a God who demands His subjects to climb higher to Him? I don't know about you, but I don't have room for a God like that.

But the beauty of the Gospel tells us that we don't have a God like that. We have a God that reached down to the lowest depths the universe has, until He became a Man and walked this forsaken earth. And He did it for each and every one of us.

Isn't that the kind of love you can respond to? The kind that you can say "I do" to?

*Some facts in this story were slightly altered to protect those involved.

NOTES

1. Gerald F. Hawthorne, *Philippians*. WBC, vol. 43 (Waco, Tex.: Word Books, 1983), 85.

2. C.F.D. Moule, "The manhood of Jesus in the New Testament," in *Christ Faith and History*, ed. S.W. Sykes and J.P. Clayton (London: Cambridge University Press, 1972), 97.

CHAPTER VII

DID JESUS HAVE A SEX DRIVE?

*"Jesus wasn't a sexless, lifeless half-man. He had sexual
urges and desires. He appreciated the beauty of women. He
noticed the beauty of women. He was really a man."*[1]

I'm sure you are intrigued by the title of this chapter,
perhaps even a little scandalized. But before we delve into
this very important discussion, let me just tell you that it is
with fear and trepidation that I write. If ever there were a
delicate topic to discuss, it is this one. To address this topic
with carelessness would be like Nadab and Abihu offering
profane fire before the Lord. And just as Moses approached
the burning bush, we must approach this chapter with our
shoes off and with a great deal of holy reverence.

Yet it is a very relevant and important topic. Fear and
reverence shouldn't turn us away from looking into it. Just
as Moses said when he saw the burning bush, "I will go near
and see this great sight" (Exodus 3:3, LXE), we must go
near to our Savior and reflect upon His nearness to us.

Enda Lyons, a Catholic priest from Ireland, astutely
noted, "It is one thing to *say* that Jesus was 'truly human.'.
[*sic*] It is another to be convinced of this and really to mean
it" (emphasis original).[2]

What we want is to be convinced of Christ's humanity.
We don't want to play lip service to this idea. It is important,
therefore, to grapple with the implications of what His
"humanness" implies. We know that the "Word became
flesh, and dwelt among us" (John 1:14); we know that
Christ was "born of a woman" (Galatians 4:4), but what
does all this mean? Is there anything in the humanity of
our Beloved Groom that would attract us to Him?

I must clarify, however, that I'm not writing this chapter
to enter into the "nature of Christ" debate. If you're not
already aware, the debate over Christ's human nature
has been heatedly going on for years within the Adventist
church. One side believes that Christ took the same human

nature that Adam possessed before he sinned, while the other side believes that Christ took the same nature Adam possessed after he sinned. Whole churches have been engaged in "civil war" over the semantics of this debate. My dad recently shared a story with me illustrating the level to which this discussion can reach.

During a recent camp meeting, my parents were walking into the Adventist Book Center when my dad stopped to talk with someone he knew. A few minutes later, my mother came running out and said, "Bill, you have to get in here. There are two men arguing quite loudly in the middle of the store." My dad immediately raced inside to find two men arguing with great zeal over the nature of Christ. Their words could be heard throughout the whole building. Finally, after seeing their fury and knowing both of them, my dad stepped in and said, "Guys, this is no place to be in such a discussion." Though the men were both very angry, one of them agreed and went to shake the other's hand, but the other man refused his attempt, turned around, and walked away.

Though there is a definite place within theological circles to lovingly and prayerfully discuss the finer points of this issue, too many times we have missed the greater truth behind the reality of Christ's humanity. As Adventists, we take this truth for granted. If you were to search through the books of non-Adventist Christians around the world, you would see that there is a huge vacuum when it comes to the beauty of Christ's identity with humanity. There is virtually no material outside of Adventism that addresses Christ's identification with sinful humanity. It's just not important to them.

Though Adventists may get downright nasty when it comes to the finer points of this truth, there is at least an emphasis on it. The Savior that Seventh-day Adventists uplift draws a lot closer to us than most other Christian churches. For that, we should be encouraged.

But we've still missed the boat, to a large extent. I don't know how many times I've sat in a Sabbath School class or other small group and heard someone discouraged about their "trials and temptations." They are plagued by a problem or disheartened by a particular sin. Sadly, most people don't have a comforting solution. They either encourage the person to "pray more" or stick their nose to the grindstone and try harder. If they speak of Jesus, they portray Him as someone who is standing on the sidelines, saying, "Rah, rah, rah. You can make it. Just stick with it."

But Christ is much closer to us than the sidelines. He's in the game.

One of the beauties in the book of Hebrews reveals the fact that Jesus is our High Priest. Just as there was a High Priest who ministered in the ancient Israelite sanctuary service, so Christ ministers on our behalf in the heavenly sanctuary right now. This fact is one of the most encouraging truths of the sanctuary doctrine.

But the author of Hebrews, who many say was the apostle Paul, didn't just leave it at that. In the second chapter of this epistle, he wrote, "For indeed [Christ] does not give aid to angels, but He does give aid to the seed of Abraham. Therefore, in all things He had to be made like His brethren, that He might be a merciful and faithful High Priest in things pertaining to God, to make propitiation for the sins of the people" (Hebrews 2:16, 17).

It's a sobering thought. Christ, the Ruler of the Universe, was made exactly like you and me. Some people may have the impression that Christ was born with a red cape on—that He was born Superman—but that's not what Hebrews tells us at all. We are told that He was "in all things" made like His brothers and sisters. He wasn't born with a silver spoon in His mouth; He didn't have any more advantage in His humanity than we do.

In fact, Christ was born with many disadvantages, perhaps some of which we are not even subject to. Not only do the chronologies presented in Matthew and Luke show a picture of a less-than-ideal family tree (if you've never taken the time to go through the names of some of Jesus' ancestors, it's a fascinating study), but Christ's immediate family situation wasn't exactly glorious. He was born in a stable, to start with. And His birth was the subject of much controversy, both in His time and throughout the centuries since.

In fact, I recently read a book titled, *The Illegitimacy of Jesus*, which proposes that Christ was conceived illegitimately as a result of an affair that Mary was having. The author insinuates that Matthew and Luke were aware of this, and they leave clues in their books that reveal such an idea. The thought is pure rubbish, of course, but to think that the circumstances of Christ's birth could even allow for such a possibility to be discussed says a lot about His condescension.

Though Christ wasn't born illegitimately, as some people may have been, we can truly take comfort in knowing that He wasn't born with any inherent advantages over us. Hebrews unequivocally tells us that He was "in all things" made like His brothers.

I can hear someone object, however, "If Christ didn't have any advantage over the rest of us, then how did He perform all of those miracles and abstain from sinning?" He, Himself, explains, "Most assuredly, I say to you, the Son can do nothing of Himself, but what He sees the Father do" (John 5:19). The power that Christ utilized to live an extraordinary life was what He acquired by faith. Elsewhere, He says, "Most assuredly, I say to you, he who believes in Me, the works that I do he will do also; and greater works than these he will do, because I go to My Father" (John 14:12). The power that Christ tapped into is the same power that we can tap into. It wasn't a power that came "built-into" His human body.

Imagine if Prince William, the much heralded and idolized English Prince, visited the slums of London and gave a speech, saying, "Be like me. Aim high. If you believe it, you can achieve it." No one would listen to him, as good-looking as he may be. Their starting points would be nowhere near the same level. Prince William was born into royalty and will probably be the King of England some day simply because of his birthrights.

This is the reason we like so-called "human interest stories." Every time the Olympics come around, we're bombarded with these types of stories. We hear about John Doe, who was brought up by his great-aunt Bertha's three-legged dog. And when we see that John has just won the 1000m speed skating gold medal, we figure that we can do it too.

Or when we hear that Bill Gates went from being a college dropout to the world's richest man, we have visions of grandeur as well. But set Prince William down in front of us, telling us the secrets of rising to the top, and it's more discouraging than encouraging. He doesn't have the foggiest idea of what it's like to live in adversity.

That's why it is so important that we recognize Christ was "in all things" made like us. God put Himself on the same playing field as His creatures. And when He encourages us to "overcome" as He "overcame" (Revelation 3:21), we realize it's not just a pie-in-the-sky idea. Christ, in His humanity, rose from obscurity to become the shining example of what humankind can achieve through His grace.

When Paul wrote that Christ was "in all things" made like His brothers, he wasn't just speaking of His physical features. It doesn't mean much for us as human beings if Christ simply had the same body parts as us. Though it is an extraordinary thought in itself—that God could put on human flesh—this is not the remarkable point that Paul is driving home.

Following the implications of Paul's reasoning, it would lead us to conclude that Christ did indeed have a "sex drive." I'm sure that this idea sounds scandalous to many people. And in light of some of the crazy theories that have been proposed over the last two thousand years, epitomized by the recent *Da Vinci Code*, we do have to be careful how far we take this. Yet Paul told us beyond a shadow of a doubt that Christ was "in all things" made like His brothers. And I've yet to meet a "brother" that wasn't born with a "sex drive." Even Adam, in his sinless state, had a "sex drive," which is nothing more than the desire to have sex.

The truth of the matter is, Christ subjected Himself to the same circumstances that we find ourselves in. And we can take comfort in this, knowing that our almighty God can identify with our experiences. This doesn't mean, however, that Christ allowed that sex drive to ever take hold of His life. Just as quickly as the thought would enter His mind, He would quickly dismiss it. He never dwelt on the idea or lusted after those sexual desires that every human being, perfect or imperfect, was made with.

But, although Christ was "in all things" made like His brothers, Hebrews even takes it a step further than that. Two chapters later we read, "For we do not have a High Priest who cannot sympathize with our weaknesses, but was in all points tempted as we are, yet without sin" (Hebrews 4:15). Not only do we have a High Priest that was "in all things" made like us, but He was "in all points tempted as we are."

Don't take this idea for granted. Although we may not give it much thought, Christ did experience the same things we do. He was a child like us. He was a teenager like us, subject to peer pressure. We may have the impression that Jesus was a social recluse and didn't have friends to tempt Him to deviate from the straight and narrow, but the truth is that He loved socializing with others. And wherever there are young boys, mischief is in the air. You don't think that Christ ever heard the lines, "Oh, come on, Jesus...just one more inning before Sabbath!"?

As He grew older and developed more, I'm sure He caught a lot of the girls' eyes. After all, He was a very nice guy: smart, dependable, polite, honest, caring, sensitive, trustworthy, and sincere. And I'm sure that He had personality. What girl wouldn't be attracted to such a guy? He was the proverbial "Knight in shining armor." Although it may seem silly to say about Him, in all sincerity, Christ was the most eligible Batchelor the planet has ever seen. No contestant on a game show could rival Him.

Truthfully, the Devil would have been stupid not to throw sexual temptation at Him. No other temptation has been the downfall for so many males throughout this earth's history as this one. Why not try to hit Christ at man's weakest point, then? Maybe in a moment of weakness He would deviate from the path.

It would be remiss of me to limit Christ's temptations to the sexual realm, of course. Hebrews tells us that He was "in all points" tempted as we are. This doesn't mean that the details of our temptations are exactly the same as that of Christ's. Obviously, He was never tempted to surf the Internet for pornography, or steal a car, or blow all of his paycheck on alcohol. But the nature of His temptations match those which we face.

Thus, He was tempted to steal (though the exact object may differ from what we're tempted to steal), covet, or murder. Satan tried to lay claim to Christ's allegiance by tempting Him to gratify self—which is the root of all sin—and diverting from the will of His Father.

To limit Christ's temptations to those that He experienced in the wilderness is to miss the point as well. Some claim that Christ's temptations were simply to utilize His divinity to His own advantage, or that Satan appealed to the natural cravings of the human body (hunger, thirst, etc.).

But limiting Christ's temptations to these things would miss Paul's point in Hebrews 4. Paul writes that Christ was "in all points tempted as we are." This is so that He could identify with humanity and so we could find a true solace in a God that knows what we're going through. It's never been a temptation to use my divinity. Nor is it all that big a deal if I have a Savior who was simply hungry just as I am hungry. The temptations that challenge me are those that I face on a daily basis—impatience, hatred, envy, coveting. I find comfort in knowing Christ faced these and was victorious over them.

That is why Paul continues, "Let us therefore come boldly to the throne of grace, that we may obtain mercy and find grace to help in time of need" (Hebrews 4:16). Because of Christ's identity with humankind, we can come with boldness and confidence to His throne. He's not going to criticize us for failing once again, having no clue what we've gone through. Because of His experience with humanity, He knows how tough the path is and how much a person needs grace. Our struggles were His struggles. Our temptations,

His temptations. Our loneliness, His loneliness. And He's ever eager to lift us up when we've fallen.

I think we try to sterilize Christ's human experience. Too many times we like to picture Jesus as a person who lived in a big castle with a moat around it and an ADT home security system. Every time some kind of difficulty or temptation would come up, God the Father would simply divert the traffic elsewhere, so Jesus never really had to face any challenges. It's justifiable then to have a picture of Christ on a stained glass window way up behind the pulpit of our churches, three hundred feet from where we are. He can't really identify with our experiences.

But this is not the Gospel at all. The Gospel is a lot better news than that. There is no trial that comes along in your experience that Christ has not also encountered. There is no temptation that the devil throws at you that Christ has not already gained the victory over. And His victory can be your victory through His grace.

I love what Isaiah 53:3 says, speaking prophetically of the Messiah: "He was despised and forsaken of men, a man of sorrows and acquainted with grief; and like one from whom men hide their face He was despised, and we did not esteem Him" (NASB). As amazing as the words are in this passage, I've yet to read a translation that truly captures the depth of meaning that the Hebrew sets forth. As much as I enjoy the poetic words of Handel's *Messiah*, they fall short.

The Hebrew word we translate as "grief" would better be translated as "disease" or "sickness." Thus, Christ had an experience that far surpassed mere grief; He encountered the horrible frailties that humankind is plagued with. Christ was not simply "acquainted" with grief or sickness. The Hebrew tells us that He knew it intimately. In fact, the word used for "acquainted" is the same word that is used for Adam "knowing" Eve sexually in Genesis 4. So it wasn't a mere acquaintance. It was an identity. He was a man of sorrows who intimately knew disease and sickness.

Christ didn't have a mere passing encounter with grief or disease. He so closely identified with them that they were a part of who He was as a human being. We don't have a Savior whose human existence was in any way exalted above ours, but we worship and follow a Christ who placed Himself in our shoes. In fact, in light of the cross, we know that He placed Himself in a lower state than any of us were ever intended to experience. Paul wrote, "For He made Him who knew no sin to be sin for us, that we might become the righteousness of God in Him" (2 Corinthians 5:21).

One of the most fascinating books I've ever read is Lance Armstrong's autobiography, *It's Not About the Bike: My Journey Back to Life*. It is one of those books that you can't put down; a real page-turner. It took me all of about 12 hours to read the whole thing—all 289 pages of it.

For those of you who aren't familiar with Lance Armstrong, he is a cyclist who won the *Tour De France*, the "Super Bowl" of bike racing, seven years in a row. Winning the *Tour* is hard enough. Winning it seven times in a row is remarkable. Winning it seven times in a row after surviving cancer, chemo-therapy and brain surgery is out of this world. That's what Lance Armstrong did.

As compelling and moving as his fight back to the top of the cycling world was, however, his identity as a cancer survivor is even more. Sure, he's won the *Tour* seven times, but he prefers to be called a "cancer survivor" rather than a cycling champion. Even though the doctors thought he had about a 3% chance of living (yes *3%*), somehow he beat the disease and is healthier than ever. He would often have "conversations with cancer" and tell the cancer that it picked the wrong body to mess with; he was going to beat it.

The most compelling tales he has to tell, though, are about his identification with other cancer patients. He will always be a cancer survivor; no one can take that away from him. And one of his greatest joys in life is talking to people who are battling the disease, hoping to encourage them in their fight.

"I had it too and I beat it," he can tell them. That right there is enough to give a 10-year-old girl encouragement and hope through it all. Realizing that this man knows what she's going through is enough to change her dark day into one filled with sunshine. Understanding that he beat the odds too gives her a hope like none other.

I'm sure that if I tried to encourage a young boy with cancer in the hospital, it would maybe make him feel a little better. But if I were to bring Lance Armstrong into his room to encourage him, it would just brighten up his day.

I have no idea what that boy is going through. I don't know what it feels like to have chemicals pumped into my bloodstream. I don't know what it feels like to lose all of my hair and have other people give me funny looks as a result. I don't know what it feels like to lie in a hospital bed, vomiting all night and wondering if I even want to live to see tomorrow.

But Lance does. Lance has been there. Lance knows what it feels like, and that would give the boy all the comfort in the world. It might even be enough to encourage that kid to look forward to another day.

Jesus is a cancer survivor, in a way. He was born with that dreadful disease called humanity, just like you and me. But He didn't let it beat Him. He didn't give in to the pressures or gloom that being human causes. He fought against those incredible odds and beat the devil at his own game. He told sin that it picked the wrong body to mess with and He "condemned sin in the flesh, that the righteous requirement of the law might be fulfilled in us" (Romans 8:3, 4).

And what does that do for me? It tells me that I can also beat those incredible odds, because Someone else has done it before me. What an incredible encouragement it is to me, someone who was born with that awful disease! Knowing that I have a Lover who went through the same struggles, yet overcame and beat the disease, I am extremely excited about my chances; things are looking up. I'm going to make it.

I'm going to make it because I have a Bridegroom who will teach me "to say 'No' to ungodliness and worldly passions, and to live [a] self-controlled, upright and godly [life] in this present age" (Titus 2:12, NIV). I'm going to make it because I have a Bridegroom who's not just standing on the sidelines, cheering me on; He's actually in the game with me. I'm extremely thankful for a Lover like that. My heart is overwhelmed with that kind of love. He didn't have to put Himself in that same, vulnerable position that I was born in. But He did.

I can't comprehend that in my feeble, human mind. What would drive a King to become a poor, helpless child like me? I don't know. All I can do is say "thank you" and continue down the road, hand-in-hand with an Awesome Guy.

NOTES

1. Joshua Harris, *Not Even a Hint* (Sisters, Ore.: Multnomah, 2003), 34, 35.
2. Enda Lyons, *Jesus: Self-Portrait by God* (New York and Mahwah, N.J.: Paulist Press, 1994), 56.

CHAPTER VIII

THIS MAN...EATS WITH SINNERS

I like to tell people that the most amazing thing about Dr. Lael Caesar is not the fact that he has a Ph. D from the University of Wisconsin; it's not the fact that he can confound you with a lecture on the meaning of *tohu vabohu*; it's not even the fact that he can pretty much pick up a new language in his sleep. The most amazing thing about Dr. Lael Caesar is the fact that he eats with sinners. Let me explain.

Dr. Caesar teaches at Andrews University in the undergraduate religion department, and although he is technically a professor of religion, he refers to himself simply as a "Bible teacher." But this "lofty" position isn't reflected in his attitude or actions. While most college professors distance themselves from students outside of the classroom, Dr. Caesar draws closer to them. If you were to see him in the cafeteria, you would notice that he is always surrounded by hordes of students as he eats lunch. He purposely sits down in the middle of a group of students and socializes with them joyfully and passionately. The sound of his laughter and happiness echoes throughout the cafeteria. He is drunk with joy.

This may not seem like a big deal to some people, but for a college student, it means the world. It's the reason that he's nominated for the "Teacher of the Year" award just about every year at Andrews. Students know that they have a friend in Dr. Caesar. He's not just a professor or an authority figure; he's someone who cares about them.

His loving attitude doesn't only show itself at the dinner table, however. I don't know how many times he would come to watch my intramural basketball or floor hockey games. In fact, one particular game he attended was quite shocking. I had told him about it the day of the game, but he, unfortunately, informed me that he wouldn't be able to attend because he had a class at the same time. But it was my championship floor hockey game, and I could see the great anguish on his face. He has, after all, always considered me to be one of his "sons."

The game started and the excitement built. The first few minutes were action filled, and I thought nothing of Dr. Caesar, assuming I would have to tell him about the result of the game at a later time. But a few minutes into the match, I all of a sudden heard a booming and magnificent voice coming from the stands, "Go, Shawn!" I looked up and, sure enough, it was Dr. Caesar.

When I talked with him later and asked him about his class, he told me that he had given his students a test and then left to come watch the game. I was quite flattered by his efforts and sacrifices. But what is even more remarkable is the fact that, in all honesty, Dr. Caesar is not even an advocate of competition. He pretty much swears it off in all forms. Yet you'll often see him in the gymnasium, cheering loudly (and when I say loudly, you can hear him above everyone else) for a multitude of people. His love for "sinners" far outweighs any opinions he may have of the activities they engage in.

He truly, in all senses of the idea, eats with sinners.

But Dr. Caesar isn't the first person to have ever eaten with sinners. Long before he was born, another Man was the target of this description. It wasn't in as positive a light, however. The Gospel of Luke shares a small thumbnail sketch of when Jesus was accused of this "heinous" activity. Luke wrote, "Then all the tax collectors and the sinners drew near to Him to hear Him" (Luke 15:1).

Obviously, Luke didn't mean that every single tax collector and every single sinner in the whole world drew near to Jesus; He was using a little hyperbole there. But he did want to emphasize the fact that there were hordes of these types of people who were drawn to Jesus. In fact, the picture Luke painted gives the impression that this wasn't a one-time situation; Luke literally said that these people were in a constant state of being drawn to Christ. They just couldn't resist Him.

We see a more detailed picture of this very idea a few chapters later. In Luke 19 we get that wonderful song we sing as children, "Zacchaeus was a wee little man, a wee little man was he..." In one of the most beautiful illustrations of Christ's love for sinners, He pursued this wretched tax collector and invited Himself over for some lunch.

Of course, the reaction from some of the "saints" was the same in that story as it was in Luke 15. In both places we read, "And the Pharisees and scribes complained, saying, 'This Man receives sinners and eats with them'" (Luke 15:2; Luke 19:7). To say that this type of behavior upset the "big-wigs" of the Jewish Religious Police is an understatement. They were absolutely scandalized by Christ's actions.

The Pharisees had strict standards when it came to so-called "table fellowship." A person was not allowed to eat with just anyone. Being religious elites, the Pharisees wanted to make sure that they were conducting their lives appropriately in every area. Not only did they strictly follow the dietary laws as prescribed in the book of Leviticus, but they piled more laws on top of those to make sure that they had room to wiggle.

Just to give you an idea of how strict some of these laws were during Jesus' time, one law, set up during the Jewish exile in Babylon, stated that two acquaintances were not allowed to sit across the table from one another if one were eating cheese and the other were eating meat. (Many of us would be in trouble at a typical potluck today, though I'm not sure if the same rules would apply to veggie-meat.) The reason for this was because some of the rabbis believed that if the two acquaintances knew each other, their thoughts would mix in the middle of the room, thus mixing milk and meat, which was against the law. However, it was all right if the two people didn't know one another because their thoughts wouldn't mix.[1]

We can look back at these ideas and laugh, but the Pharisees in Jesus' day wanted to keep the letter of the law. To some extent, we should cut them some slack. Their intentions were fairly pure. They understood that the Israelite nation had fallen into exile because they had not stayed faithful to God. Thus, they figured that if they could just keep the law down to the minutest detail, they could avoid ever finding themselves in exile again. They took it upon themselves to be the Religious Police, and Christ was violating their laws by eating with sinners and tax collectors.

At the same time, it's somewhat easy to see why the Pharisees, and the Jewish people as a whole, held such a disdain for tax collectors. They worked for the Roman government. As Kenneth E. Bailey wrote, "Only one who has been privileged to be a part of a community living under military occupation can fully understand the feelings of such a community toward the 'collaborator.'" He compares it to French collaborators during the time of Nazi occupation that were killed or imprisoned after the war was over; or collaborators in South Africa who "were burned to death with rubber tires and gasoline." Still, one Jewish man who survived the Warsaw ghetto during World War II admitted that a number of Jewish collaborators were butchered by their fellow Jews before the ghettos fell.[2]

Yet, in spite of the great disdain for the sinners and tax collectors, Jesus ate with these people. He welcomed these people. When the rest of the Jewish nation looked down their noses at these "sinners," Jesus drew closer to them and fellowshipped with them.

Thus, in response to the scribes and Pharisees' complaints, Jesus shared three stories in Luke 15 that reveal the heart of His mission. In these three stories—which I like to call the "Lost and Found Trilogy"—Christ expounded upon the initiative of His loving Father. There we see the ultimate picture of what God is truly like.

Though all three of the parables are rich with meaning, my favorite is the first one that Jesus shared. Immediately after the scribes and Pharisees complained, Luke wrote, "So He spoke this parable to them, saying, 'What man of you, having a hundred sheep, if he loses one of them, does not leave the ninety-nine in the wilderness, and go after the one which is lost until he finds it?'" (Luke 15:3, 4).

For Jesus' listening audience, the imagery wasn't farfetched at all. In fact, the scribes and Pharisees, who were well-versed in the Hebrew scriptures, would have immediately tied Jesus' parable to a few passages in the writings of the Old Testament. Ezekiel recorded the Lord as saying, "Son of man, prophesy against the shepherds of Israel, prophesy and say to them, 'Thus says the Lord God to the shepherds, "Woe to the shepherds of Israel who feed themselves!' " (Ezekiel 34:2). A few verses later, the Lord continued, "So [my sheep] were scattered because there was no shepherd...My sheep wandered through all the mountains, and on every high hill; yes, My flock was scattered over the whole face of the earth, and no one was seeking or searching for them" (Ezekiel 34:5, 6).

The religious leaders Jesus was talking to understood the correlation, no doubt. Jesus was giving them a direct indictment as to their failure to take care of the flock. They were the shepherds of Israel who failed to watch over and care for the sheep. Just as the shepherds in Ezekiel were responsible for allowing the Lord's sheep to "wander," so too were the scribes and Pharisees responsible for allowing the "sinners" to wander aimlessly without a shepherd in Jesus' day.

But the message in Ezekiel didn't end there, nor did it end in Jesus' story. Because of the shepherds' irresponsibility in Ezekiel, the Lord continued, "For thus says the Lord God, 'Indeed, I Myself will search for My sheep, and seek them out...I will seek what was lost and bring back what was driven away, bind up the broken and strengthen what was sick," (Ezekiel 34:11, 16). In the unfolding of Christ's parable, He revealed to the Pharisees that He was the fulfillment of this very prophecy.

But not only that, Christ also wanted to show that He was making up for the scribes and Pharisees' failures. Where they failed, He was picking up the slack. In essence, He was saying, "You are the ones who are supposed to be caring for the sheep. I'm simply doing your job; and all you do is complain about it."

The endings of Christ's three parables reveal a direct contrast between the attitude toward the lost sheep of Israel, as well. While the scribes and Pharisees complained about the outcasts, Christ made it clear that all of heaven rejoices over these lost souls that are brought back into the fold. "There will be more rejoicing in heaven over one sinner who repents," Jesus said, "than over ninety-nine just persons who need no repentance" (Luke 15:7).

But the deep truths that Christ revealed in this parable don't end there. More than just berating the Pharisees for their failures at tending the flock, Christ revealed the very heart of God and the initiative He takes in seeking the lost. In the story of Zacchaeus a few chapters later, we read Jesus' well-known words, "For the Son of Man has come to seek and to save that which was lost" (Luke 19:10).

The parable of the lost sheep spells that out plainly. Jesus, in pointing to Himself, declared that He would "go after" the one lost sheep "until he finds it" (Luke 15:4). This is the story of redemption. This is Christ's mission to the world. It is His job to seek; it is His job to save.

Some of us have the impression that it is *our* job to do the seeking. We quote or sing passages that say, "Seek ye first the kingdom of God..." thinking that if we just search and look hard enough, we will be able to find our way home. But Christ declares in this parable that *He* is the one seeking.

No passage in scripture tells the story of a sheep looking for the shepherd. With all due respect, I haven't encountered very many smart sheep, either. They're pretty dumb animals. I'm willing to say that it is almost *impossible* for a sheep, once it is lost, to find its way home. They just don't have it in their cognitive makeup to retrace their steps back to the fold.

But the beauty of the Gospel tells us that we don't have to worry about finding our way home. Jesus worries about that. Jesus searches high and low until He finds that which is lost. All of scripture testifies of this. We see a picture of a searching God, not only in the life of Christ, but in the Old Testament as well.

What Christ was doing then, by welcoming and eating with sinners, was taking the initiative in their relationship. That's what He did with Zacchaeus. He didn't wait for Zacchaeus to invite Him over for lunch; Luke told us that Jesus came to the little tree that Zacchaeus had climbed and said, "Zacchaeus, hurry down. Today is my day to be a guest in your home" (Luke 19:5, *The Message*).

What was Zacchaeus' response? I love how Eugene Peterson renders it, "Zacchaeus scrambled out of the tree, hardly believing his good luck, delighted to take Jesus home with him" (v. 6). Here was a man who couldn't believe the Lord's loving initiative. The Savior actively sought an audience with him in his home.

Maybe you haven't been as fortunate as Zacchaeus. Maybe the Jesus that has been presented to you isn't the type who approaches your tree and seeks admittance into your home. But whether or not this Jesus has been presented to you, this is the Jesus of scripture. Indeed, this is the God of scripture. He is ever seeking after us. This is the biggest difference between the God we serve and the gods of other religions. Whereas the gods of other religions are unapproachable, our God is not only approachable, He is the one who does the approaching.

Although it may not be an easy thing to do, it would be good for us to stop thinking that we're the ones who need to make the first move when it comes to our walk with Christ. This type of thinking only produces discouragement. It's hard for us to fall in love with a Groom if we have to do all the work in the relationship.

Unfortunately, I learned this lesson in my courting days with my wife. There were a few times when she was putting all the work into the relationship, while I was taking no initiative whatsoever. I was a very poor reflection of the Groom I claim to model my life after. As a result of my inefficiencies, Camille became very discouraged about our relationship, and there was one particular time that we almost called it quits altogether.

Fortunately, God woke me up to my calling as the initiator, and we slowly mended the relationship. It's a lot easier for a young lady to be excited about her man when he is initiating in the relationship. My excitement for Camille produces an excitement in her life for me. God never intended for it to be the other way around, largely because He desired our human relationships to be a reflection of His relationship with us. He, the Groom, is the initiator; we, the bride, merely respond to His overtures.

Thus, we see a picture in the scriptures of God pursuing His bride. He takes the initiative in the relationship. He seeks after us. And that seeking will produce a response in our hearts. His excitement for us will be echoed as an excited response towards Him. We don't have to produce the excitement on our own; there is no such thing as a "self-starter" when it comes to man's relation to God.

This is the very reason that Christ ate with sinners. He was taking the initiative in the relationship and hoping to draw a response from them. And He does the same with us. As we saw before, Revelation quotes Jesus as saying, "Behold, I stand at the door, and knock: if any man hear my voice, and open the door, I will come in to him, and will sup with him, and he with me" (Revelation 3:20, KJV).

Christ is standing at our doors, knocking. He's taking the initiative in the courtship days. And He wants admittance into our hearts. Why? Because He wants to "sup" with us; He wants to eat with us, the sinners that we are.

Are you tired of searching for God? Have you had trouble finding the Love of your life? Stop looking. Stop seeking. That lovely Groom is searching for you. And He will search for you "until He finds" you.

NOTES

1. Kenneth E. Bailey, *Finding the Lost: Cultural Keys to Luke 15* (St. Louis: Concordia Publishing House, 1992), 60.
2. Ibid., 61.

CHAPTER IX

SEPARATION

It's a cool spring evening in the Middle East. A gentle breeze caresses the hillsides that surround Jerusalem. In the distance we can see the countryside illuminated by the light of the moon. All is quiet after a long day. People have settled in for the night.

But then as we listen a little more intently, we hear a bloodcurdling cry coming from the outskirts of the city. It doesn't sound good, to say the least. We slowly make our way toward the sound, worried that something horrific has happened. As we inch closer, we notice three men lying face down on the ground. We're not sure if they're sleeping or if they're dead. The cry gets louder as we get closer. As we round a bend, we expect to see a fist fight going on, maybe even a brutal slaying. Surely two people are violently wrestling with one another, struggling for their lives.

But as we turn the corner, we see a most unusual sight. There in front of us is a single man. He is all alone. And yet we get the profound impression that he is not. At least he certainly isn't acting as if he is. Maybe that has to do with the fact that he is covered with blood.

What is wrong with this man? Has he gone mad? Is he fighting with demons? Who is he speaking to? Is he schizophrenic?

No. He's not schizophrenic. He has not gone mad. He is not fighting with demons, so to speak. He is, in fact, struggling with God. His name is Jesus.

There in the Garden of Gethsemane is a man claiming to be God. He has lived on this earth for more than 30 years, traveling Palestine and causing a scene wherever He goes. He has made deaf people hear; He has caused the blind to see; He has fed 5,000 people with a few morsels of food; He's preached about some pretty radical things. Everything He has done has been discussed far and near.

And yet here He is: a troubled soul, seemingly on the edge of a nervous breakdown.

It is quite humbling to see God in a garden, pleading for His own life. We sometimes rush over those scenes in the garden too quickly. The words don't necessarily take life when we read them in the Gospel accounts. But they are rich with meaning if we tarry beside them for a few minutes.

After a final Passover supper in the upper room, Jesus led His disciples to Gethsemane. It had been a place He had frequented with them to spend a few moments in prayer and reflection. This time was different, however; Jesus' steps didn't appear to have as much confidence as usual. His words weren't as assertive. Something seemed to be bothering Him. The disciples, despite the fact that Jesus had only told them about 500 times what was about to take place, didn't catch on to what was happening.

Still, Jesus pressed on toward His favorite place in the garden. He seemed eager to find solace there. Stopping, He invited Peter, James, and John to especially continue on with Him. Because the three were His closest disciples, He deeply desired to have their companionship during this most tumultuous occasion. So they continued with Him as far as He allowed.

In the journey, however, He perplexingly remarked to them, "My soul is exceedingly sorrowful, even to death" (Matthew 26:38). This, no doubt, confused the three disciples. What on earth was He talking about? Was He not going to soon establish His kingdom on earth? They shrugged it off.

And then, after encouraging them to stay and pray for both Him and themselves, Jesus walked on alone.

Jesus, of course, had always felt alone on this earth, humanly speaking. Although He was constantly surrounded by other people, He was profoundly alone. He was different from them. But, no matter how alone He had felt at times, He always felt the presence of His Father and other ministering beings.

Now He was really alone. In the absence of divine companionship, from which He felt separated, He now desired human companionship. And that's why He encouraged His closest disciples to stay close by His side. How little they provided that companionship for Him though. In the most important and traumatic moment in Jesus' life, His disciples—the closest friends He had—quickly fell asleep. They fell infinitely short of the support Jesus needed most. These were the same guys who, hours before, swore that they would always be there for Jesus. These were the guys who boasted of their allegiance to Him.

So Jesus fell to the ground, weighted down by the tremendous burden He felt on His shoulders. He knew the prophecies in the Old Testament. He knew how, hundreds of years earlier, Isaiah wrote of Him, "Surely He has borne our griefs and carried our sorrows" (Isaiah 53:4). It was happening to Him right then and there. He was carrying those sorrows for sure. It was overwhelming.

We must allow Jesus, though perfect, to have a moment of resistance. We must allow Him to wrestle with God. We would be left wondering how much of a sacrifice it really was if Jesus had simply gone through the whole ordeal smiling and un-conflicted.

And so that's what Jesus did. He agonized over the process. It wasn't a man named John Smith or Mike Jones or Dave Brown playing the part in a movie, realizing full well that he would soon be back in his trailer, sipping an iced tea. It wasn't a friend of yours or mine who was acting in a "passion play," struggling to remember to say the right lines and portray the scripted emotion that would convey the seriousness of the scene to the audience. It was really Jesus. And He was really struggling.

It's no wonder that He, the suffering Servant foretold by Isaiah, cried out with great emotion and tears in His voice, "O, My Father, if it is possible, let this cup pass from Me." Perhaps the seriousness of these words doesn't jump out at us from the written page. Perhaps we've heard them so many times that we're immune to their significance. But Jesus screamed them with tears leaping out of His eyes. His piercing voice echoed throughout the garden.

A casual observer wouldn't understand the gravity of what He was experiencing. Maybe our "trained" Christian eye even fails to see just what He was going through. To put it simply, God and sin were at war with one another. There in the Garden of Gethsemane Jesus was experiencing what God does to sin. The two cannot exist side by side.

Some people have the impression that God is so gracious and loving that He can be in the presence of sin without "all hell breaking loose" (in a real and literal sense). A story like the prodigal son, where we see a father who eagerly and willingly welcomes back his sinful and wretched son, leads us to believe that God has no problem with unrighteousness and will ignore it forever. As the English theologian John Stott wrote, "The kind of God who appeals to most people today would be easygoing in his tolerance of our offences."[1]

But this couldn't be further from the truth. God cannot be in the presence of evil. He is holy, and everything about sin is the exact opposite of His character. Just as it is impossible for darkness to exist in the presence of light, so it is impossible for sin to exist in the presence of God. As John 1:5 says, in reference to Jesus, "The light shines through the darkness, and the darkness can never extinguish it" (NLT).

This is why, in the Old Testament, we read numerous accounts of human beings that could not physically stand in God's presence and look at Him. When Moses asked God to see His glory, for example, God answered by saying, "You cannot see My face; for no man shall see Me and live" (Exodus 33:20). Instead, Moses stood in the cleft of a rock, and God placed His hand over Moses' eyes. When God passed by, Moses was then allowed to see God's back. To see God's face would have been committing suicide. Moses, a sinful man, would have met sure death.

It's little wonder then that Jesus was struggling in the garden. It's little wonder why He pleaded with His Father to take the "cup" away from Him. Paul told us elsewhere that Jesus was made "to be sin for us" (2 Corinthians 5:21). He was made to be something that His Father, who had previously referred to Jesus as being "daily His delight" (Proverbs 8:30), could not associate with anymore. Even more, it was now time for God to fix the sin problem, and the blame was placed on Jesus' shoulders. After a companionship that had existed from eternity past, it was now all coming to an end.

Think of the weight of that last statement. In our human experience we lament when relationships come to a crashing halt. Maybe we've had a boyfriend or girlfriend for a few years who has just broken up with us, or our spouse of 30 years has died. How much pain do we feel? Yet Jesus, who had always known the loving delightfulness of God the Father—for all *eternity*—was now going to be separated from Him.

This is clearly seen in Jesus' reference to the cup. It was a symbol for God's fury that would be poured out on the unrighteous. We read in Psalm 75:8, "For a cup is in the hand of the Lord, and the wine foams; it is well mixed, and He pours out of this; surely all the wicked of the earth must drain and drink down its dregs" (NASB). Again, we read in Isaiah 51:22, "Thus says your Lord, the Lord and your God, who pleads the cause of His people: 'See, I have taken out of your hand the cup of trembling, the dregs of the cup of My fury; you shall no longer drink it.'"

This is why Jesus pleaded with His Father, "O My Father, if it is possible, let this cup pass from Me" (Matthew 26:39). The cup of God's fury that the Israelite nation would "no longer" drink in Isaiah 51:22 was now in the hands of Jesus. It was there for Him to drink. He would take the full punishment for sin so that no one else would have to.

The weight of this was so overwhelming on Jesus' shoulders, in fact, that Luke told us "an angel appeared to Him from heaven, strengthening Him" (Luke 22:43). The implication is that had the angel not come to minister to Jesus, He would have never made it out of the garden alive. He would have never even seen the cross; this, in spite of the fact that no one had physically laid a hand upon Him.

But, although the angel strengthened Him, we are still told that "His sweat became like great drops of blood falling down to the ground" (Luke 22:42). To think that someone could be so emotionally overwhelmed that he actually sweats drops of blood is baffling. It's nothing I've seen before; nor is it something God ever intended man to experience. But lest we think that this was some kind of divine hyperbole, let us remember that the author of this statement, Luke, was a medical doctor. He knew what he was talking about. It's no wonder that he was the only one of the four Gospel writers to share this insight.

Modern science has confirmed what Luke reported as well. Jesus did indeed suffer from a real medical condition that, though rare, does plague people even today. The condition, now known as hematidrosis, occurs when people are under extreme mental stress, resulting in the emission of blood into a person's sweat. This happens as the result of tiny capillaries in the sweat glands that burst. In modern instances of this condition, doctors have noted that "acute fear and intense mental contemplation were found to be the most frequent inciting causes."[2]

But the modern occurrences of this medical condition pale in comparison to the hematidrosis that Jesus experienced in the garden. In the shadows of Calvary, Jesus experienced the worst medical condition a human being has ever experienced. There was no medical cure for His disease. Only the cross awaited Him. There certainly was "acute fear" and "intense mental contemplation" on Jesus' mind.

Although Christ somehow made it through that painful night in Gethsemane, He was once again thrown into the arms of God's fury the next day. Hanging on the cross, He felt the greatest offensive attack the universe has ever felt against sin. Never mind the physical pain that He was subjected to. Mere human hands couldn't cause the immeasurable pain that Christ felt; this could only come from the hands of the Almighty. The same infinite hands that formed the first man out of dust and clay could only be powerful enough to cause this Man to experience the infinite suffering and humiliation that He did.

And so Christ hung there, alone once again. This time, however, He was naked. It is fitting, then, that the wicked who perish in the end and experience hell are described as being naked (see Revelation 16:15). It is the ultimate sign of forsakenness. How appropriate for Job to say that hell "is naked before God, destruction lies uncovered" (Job 28:6, NIV).

As Jesus hung there on the cross, the Messianic prophecy of Psalm 22 was being played out right before the onlookers' eyes. Despite being written by David a thousand years before the cross, the words he wrote are the greatest description of what Christ experienced that Friday afternoon. There, on the cross, naked and alone, Jesus cried out with a loud voice, "Eloi, Eloi, lama sabachthani?" The gripping words shrieked across the hills, "My God, My God, why have You forsaken Me?" Pain was ripping His heart apart.

Some might discount Christ's words as being merely superficial. He was only acting the part, merely fulfilling prophecy. Jesus wasn't really experiencing infinite pain because He knew He would be resurrected.

But that was the dilemma Christ was going through. He knew the prophecies intellectually; He even plainly told His disciples a few days before, in reference to Himself, "They will mock Him, and scourge Him, and spit on Him, and kill Him. And the third day He will rise again" (Mark 10:34). He *knew* that He would see His Father again.

But even though Christ knew the prophecies, His heart told Him the opposite. His feelings told Him that He was never going to live again, never going to see His Father's face. Every part of His being convinced Him that this was truly the end. It wasn't simply an act. Jesus felt the infinite weight of the world's sins upon His shoulders. He truly felt the pain of separation from God.

Yet, in spite of the fact that these overwhelming feelings caused immense despondency to Jesus' heart and soul, He still held on, by faith, to the idea that He was somehow going to see His Father again. It was this faint glimmer of hope that He clung to.

Thus, in this moment of faith Jesus cried out: "Father, into Your hands I commit My spirit" (Luke 23:46). Having said this, Luke told us that He breathed His last. The last page of Christ's short life on earth was completed. His mission, as He had alluded to, was finished.

Then, in a divine fit of rage, all hell broke loose, in a real and literal sense. The veil of the temple tore in two. The earth shook and rocks split. For the first time in the history of the universe, God was being torn away from God. What ensued has never happened before; nor will it ever happen again. A new encounter was introduced that had somehow slipped the experience of the all-knowing, all-powerful, all-encompassing godhead. It was an unfamiliar sphere, even to them.

Separation.

NOTES

1. John R. W. Stott, *The Cross of Christ* (Downers Grove, Ill.: InterVarsity Press, 1986), 108.

2. http://www.apologeticspress.org/articles/2223

CHAPTER X

Have you ever experienced separation? The question is almost silly, I know. Anyone who is human has experienced it. We've all said our fair share of good-byes, or perhaps wished we had after a loved one has passed away without receiving our farewells. But have you really, truly experienced separation?

I have.

A year before my wife and I got married, we experienced separation in full force. Three weeks before I was going to return with her to Andrews University and attend the seminary, I got a call to pastor in Vermont for a year. After a lot of prayer and seeking counsel from others, I decided that the opportunity couldn't be passed up, even at the expense of being apart from Camille for at least a year.

The last few weeks of our time together we spent on family vacation in Nova Scotia, Canada, where my whole extended family owns a home. Although it was an enjoyable time, we knew what lay ahead. Our time together would inevitably have to come to an end. So after driving Camille over 1500 miles to Michigan, we made our way to a retreat center 45 minutes away from Berrien Springs, where Camille had to attend a retreat for her work. As long as the 1500 miles to Berrien Springs was, those 45 minutes to the retreat center were even longer.

The drop off was even harder. Saying good-bye is never easy, but it was even more difficult in those circumstances. Amidst the weeping that Camille was actively participating in, we managed to have a prayer and finally tear apart from one another.

But something strange happened the moment I started walking away. With Camille already out of sight, tears started streaming from my eyes. For the first time in over ten years, I started crying. The tears didn't quickly subside, though; they kept coming. I cried and cried and cried. In fact, I cried for the whole 45-minute car ride back to Berrien Springs. Never before had I felt such pain. It was so sharp. My heart was overwhelmed with grief.

Yet mere separation wasn't what caused most of the pain. We had certainly been separated before. We had certainly said good-bye and been apart from one another for significant periods of time before. To be sure, it was never as long as that year potentially was going to be; but even a long period of separation can be handled when one knows there is going to be another tomorrow.

What pained my heart the most was the unknown: the questions. In all honesty, we weren't sure if we would survive the year. Although we had gone to great lengths to try to make sure that God was leading in our relationship, there were moments of instability in our time together. We were faced with the possibility that the year apart would be the death of our relationship.

No wonder I was overwhelmed with tears. During the previous year and a half, Camille and I had spent most of our waking time together. In the light of this good-bye possibly marking the death of our relationship, all those memories flooded to my mind. They seemed as if they would be all for nothing and inevitably lost. The pain of separation and the fear of losing what we had for so long enjoyed were overwhelming to me.

It's quite sobering though: separation and the unknown. I'm sure you've gone through similar experiences yourself. Yet as painful as these experiences may be for us, we can't pretend to have any idea as to how painful it was for Christ. Separation may be a regular occurrence for us when it comes to our most important human relationships, yet Christ's separation from His Father that day was a completely new status for their relationship. They had never gone through that before.

More significant, however, is the fact that Christ truly experienced the unknown. There were questions in His mind. Doubts flooded His heart. He didn't believe the relationship with His Father was going to survive, or, at best, it would never be the same. He would forever be considered an outcast and the Person whom He admired most would look at Him with a disdaining eye. He, after all, was made "to be sin" (2 Corinthians 5:21), the very thing that His Father had no mercy for.

This is what weighed heavily upon the mind of Jesus. This is what literally broke His heart. But what perhaps added the greatest insult to injury was that the people for whom He was dying appeared to be ungrateful. All of the pain and suffering and agony were for nothing. Not only was the wrath of His Father placed upon His shoulders, but the scorn and ungratefulness of the world were thrown at Him too. He was despised.

Indeed, as the Song of Solomon so poignantly reveals, "If a Man were to give all the wealth of His house for love, He would be utterly despised" (Song of Songs 8:7; author's translation). Christ gave more than all the wealth of His house for love; He gave Himself. This is the tremendously expensive dowry He paid for the right to His bride's hand in marriage. Yet, are you going to despise Him for it?

CHAPTER XI

"WHY?"

In moments of pain and personal tragedy, it is not uncharacteristic for us to ask, "why?" In fact, this is probably the most often asked question that comes from the hearts and lips of human beings. We turn to God in search of the answers.

We are not alone. Long before we were ever asked the question, Jesus asked the same thing. Christ cried out, "My God, My God, why have You forsaken Me?" While the pain of the sins of the whole world was on His shoulders, the question that weighed heaviest upon His heart was "why?"

And it's something we could very well wonder too. Why did God forsake Jesus? And, even more basic, why did Jesus have to experience the pain of the cross in the first place?

The truth is, many times we take Jesus' death on the cross for granted. Perhaps we've even been jaded by the stories of Calvary and the reasons for it. We have our canned answers that we learned in Sabbath School as five-year-olds. We know that Jesus died for us so that we can live in heaven forever.

But have you ever taken the time to really look beyond the surface? The death of Christ is the greatest science the world has ever encountered. The truths that lie behind its vivid imagery are limitless. We will ever be learning more and more about this unmatched act of love throughout eternity. There is much to be experienced through an examination of the cross. The study of it enlightens the mind and overjoys the heart.

But, although the reasons for the cross are infinite, I want to look at three aspects of Christ's death that I believe stand above the rest. These aspects of the cross aren't simply an intellectual exercise, however. They present a picture of a Groom that should be enough to sweep a bride off her feet, certainly enough to compel her to open the door to the knocking Savior.

And so we must humbly bow before the cross and ask why.

REVELATION OF LOVE

Philip Yancey, in his book, *What's So Amazing About Grace?* shares a story of when Karl Barth, perhaps the most influential theologian of the 20th century, visited the University of Chicago. During a press conference, one astute individual asked, "Dr. Barth, what is the most profound truth you have learned in your studies?" Without hesitation, Barth replied, "Jesus loves me, this I know, for the Bible tells me so."[1]

It seems like such a simple thought. It's one of the first things we learn as young children in Sabbath School. Yet, even though those words so easily resound through our minds, their reality doesn't always sink in. How quickly we forget this idea when push comes to shove! And, as simple as the words may be, the thought is also the most profound mystery.

The cross was Jesus' way of showing His love for the world. As John wrote, "This is how we know what love is: Jesus Christ laid down his life for us" (1 John 3:16, NIV). Christ loves the world so much that He went to the cross to prove it. He wasn't like the young man who e-mailed his girlfriend one day, saying, "I love you so much. I would climb the highest mountain for you, swim the deepest ocean or walk across a hot desert. I love you, I love you, I love you. Love, Mark." Although those words would certainly cause any young lady's heart to jump, he added, "PS. I'll be over to see you tonight if it doesn't rain."

The young man was all talk and no action. His actions didn't match his words. His love was actually quite shallow. He *sounded* like a man who could rival the great romantics the world has witnessed, but when it came down to it, he didn't want to be inconvenienced by a little adversity. His love was only skin deep.

Christ's love was more than mere words, however. The cross showed that His actions could match His words. In fact, His actions far exceeded His words. His death on the cross revealed that His love for the world far exceeded the value He placed on His own life. He would rather save humankind than preserve Himself. To be sure, the Devil repeatedly tried to deter Christ from accomplishing His mission, but in the end, love won out. As we noted in the previous chapter, Christ gave "all the wealth of His house for love" (Song of Songs 8:7). Indeed, He gave Himself.

But Christ's sacrificial love moves beyond our human definition of love. Christ didn't simply die for the drop-dead gorgeous bride He hoped to marry one day; He died for the homely-looking girl that no one cared for. And even more than that, His love compelled Him to die for those who were outright enemies of His. As Romans 5:8 says, "But God demonstrates His own love toward us, in that while we were still sinners, Christ died for us." Paul declared that when we had no value whatsoever and were in enmity towards God, Christ demonstrated His incredible love by dying for us.

The cross moves beyond Christ, however. As one of my professors pointed out in a chapel talk, "No Christian ever doubts the love of Jesus." At first I was a little perplexed at what she meant by this thought, but her next statement clarified her line of reasoning when she said, "But the love of the Father is another question."

Indeed, the Christian world has always painted the picture of an incredibly loving and kindhearted Jesus. It is hard for anyone to doubt His unconditional love and forgiveness. But when it comes to God the Father, it's another story altogether. Jesus and the Father are almost seen in opposition to one another, especially in light of Jesus feeling forsaken by His Father as He hung on the cross.

But the cross was as much a revelation of the Father's love as it was Christ's. We take the words of the most well-known passage of scripture for granted, "For *God* so loved the world, that *He gave* His only begotten Son, that whosoever believeth in Him should not perish, but have everlasting life" (John 3:16, KJV; italics supplied). This text is a statement about the Father's incredible love, even more than Christ's, though the two are equal. After all, it was Jesus who declared, "He who has seen Me has seen the Father" (John 14:9). Christ's love is the Father's love. They are one and the same.

Calvary was God's majestic demonstration of love. It was the grand and glorious climax of His symphony of grace.

ACT OF SUBSTITUTION

What would you think if your spouse, or significant other, came to you one day and said, "I love you so much that I'm going to kill myself!" Although you would perhaps be flattered at first by this declaration of love, you would probably in the end think he or she was a little crazy, rather than loving. Perhaps you would even recommend some medication for him or her to take.

Truthfully, ending one's life for no good reason is more unloving than loving. As theologian John Stott writes, "If you were to jump off the end of a pier and drown, or dash into a burning building and be burnt to death, and if your self-sacrifice had no saving purpose, you would convince me of your folly, not your love." He adds, "[Christ's] death must be seen to have had an objective, before it can have an appeal."[2]

Although Christ's death on the cross certainly reveals God's heart of love, in order for it to be seen as a loving act, it had to accomplish something to begin with. Going through intense pain is more insane than loving if it doesn't achieve anything. It's called masochism.

But this is precisely where many people leave the cross. There is no reason for it in their minds, other than to reveal the character of God. But, left to itself, the cross could never reveal God's loving character without any objective mission. It would simply reveal a demented, perhaps even infatuated Groom, rather than a loving one.

Truth be told, what makes Christ's act on Calvary so loving is the fact that He died in our place. He was, in theological terms that we've probably heard before, our substitute. This idea is all too vividly illustrated by one story that took place at the Auschwitz concentration camp during the Holocaust, one of the darkest moments in human history. "When a number of prisoners were selected for execution," wrote John Stott, "one of them shouted that he was a married man with children." At this, a Catholic Priest named Maximilian Kolbe stepped forward and asked if he could be executed in the man's place. The authorities granted Kolbe's request, and he was placed in an underground cell, where he died of starvation.[3]

Such actions seem superhuman, and, in fact, they probably are, but it's exactly what Christ did. He didn't merely die to demonstrate His love; He died in place of other deserving people. This is the message that Isaiah 53 is saturated with. Speaking of Christ, Isaiah wrote, "But He was wounded for our transgressions, He was bruised for our iniquities; the chastisement for our peace was upon Him, and by His stripes we are healed" (Isaiah 53:5). Isaiah so clearly points out that the Messiah was wounded "for *our* transgressions" and bruised "for *our* iniquities." He was suffering the penalty of other peoples' actions. Sinful humanity deserved to die, but He took our place. He was our substitute.

The Apostle Paul echoed this idea in his second letter to the Corinthians. There, he wrote, "For the love of Christ compels us, because we judge thus: that if One died for all, then all died" (2 Corinthians 5:14). The mystery of the cross is that when Christ died, He died in place of humanity. And when He died there that Friday afternoon, all of humankind was placed in Him.

As was noted earlier, this tremendous action of the cross wasn't simply an experience that Christ went through alone; the Father played a part in this substitutionary work as well. He ultimately had to decide whose life—His beloved Son's or His beloved children's—He was going to take. There, on the cross, the Father gave His answer.

It reminds me of a tragic story I read about in the wake of Hurricane Ivan in 2004. The town of Cleveland, Georgia was flooded with water, and one father was faced with an unenviable decision. While the flood waters were rising to his waist, Rhys Terrill held on tightly to a tree branch with one hand and his seventeen-year-old daughter with his other. His six-year-old daughter, Cheyene, was nowhere to be found, however. She had been swept away by the surging flood waters.

His first instinct was to go look for her. What father wouldn't have this thought? But he would have had to let go of his older daughter, who would no doubt be swept away by the waters instead. In essence, he had to choose between his two daughters, a task that no parent should have to face.

"As I was holding on to my oldest," Terrill later said, "I felt my youngest slipping away from me." Indeed, Cheyene was found the next day by rescue workers, dead in a drainpipe. She was one of the youngest lives that Ivan claimed.[4]

That father's agonizing decision matched the one that God had to make. He couldn't hold onto our hand and Christ's at the same time. In order for us to be saved, He had to let go of His beloved Son. He had to let Jesus die in our place.

MISSION ACCOMPLISHED

Perhaps the greatest news of the Gospel, however, is realizing how much Christ accomplished through His death. The message of the Bible reveals that Christ didn't simply die for those who would ultimately accept His gift of salvation; He died for everyone, and everyone died in Him.

As we noted earlier, Paul wrote that "if One died for all, then all died" (2 Corinthians 5:14). The only variable in that statement is the word "if." And the word "if" is tied in with Christ's death, not its accomplishment. We know that there are no "ifs, ands, or buts" about Christ's death. He did indeed die. We can therefore conclude that everyone died in Him.

That "all" that Paul spoke of, whether you know it or not, included you. Long before you ever asked Him, or even had a choice in the matter, Christ died your death. Elsewhere Paul confirmed this by saying that Christ tasted death "for everyone" (Hebrews 2:9). Some try to limit the "everyone" to "some," specifically only those who believe or accept the gift. But this is not what the Bible teaches about Christ's death. The Bible teaches that when Christ died, He secured justification for the whole world, you and me included.

We see this spelled out in Isaiah 53, a chapter we've often referred to in this book. There, Isaiah wrote, "By His knowledge My righteous Servant shall justify many" (Isaiah 53:11). Once again, however, most, if not all, English versions don't translate this verse correctly. The actual Hebrew says that the Servant would justify "*the* many" instead of simply "many." (For a similar example of this in the New Testament, see Romans 5:15.)

Although it may seem like a subtle difference, it is a difference that changes the message of the passage greatly. Whereas "many" simply refers to a limited number of people, "*the* many" implies everyone; unless one believes that this is referring to a specific group of people that are predestined to be saved, which doesn't seem likely.

Perhaps the concept is a little confusing to you. So let me share an illustration with you that may clarify it a little bit.

Every year at Christmas time, one member of our family is particularly challenging to shop for. Do you know what I'm talking about? No matter what we buy for this person, he or she seems to want to return the present we have placed under the tree. Inevitably, this person will ask for the receipt and want to return the gift to the store the next day. It can be very frustrating! Perhaps this resonates with you.

However, just because this person doesn't appreciate or even want the gift doesn't make it any less his or hers. The minute we purchase it for this person and put it under the tree with his or her name on it, it is that person's. If the person doesn't want it, he or she can go through the hassle of getting the receipt, driving to the store, standing in a line with 237 other people returning their gifts, and get a refund. It would almost seem easier to simply keep the gift, wouldn't it?

This is precisely what Christ accomplished on His cross. He purchased the gift for everyone and placed it under the tree with our names on it. No questions asked; no strings attached. Ultimately, however, we are faced with the reality of what we're going to do with that gift—be appreciative of it or return it to the store. Sadly, most people will choose the latter option in the end.

SUMMARY

The good news of Calvary reveals many things. In the cross we see the apex of God's demonstration of love. There we understand His character. But this love is only understood when we first realize the objective aspects of Christ's death: He died in our place as a substitute, thus procuring justification for the whole world.

When we understand these concepts, our hearts truly burn within us for the Lover of our souls. The Groom that seeks after us is more loving than we first imagined or could ever have dreamed of.

NOTES

1. Philip Yancey, *What's So Amazing About Grace?* (Grand Rapids, Mich.: Zondervan, 1997), 67.

2. Stott, 220.

3. Ibid., 136.

4. Russ Bynum, "Father agonizes after Ivan claims girl," *Boston Sunday Globe*, 19 Sept. 2004, A24.

CHAPTER XII

Hillary Clinton is credited with saying, "In the Bible it says they asked Jesus how many times you should forgive, and he said 70 times seven. Well, I want you all to know that I'm keeping a chart." While she should certainly be applauded for her knowledge of the Bible, she probably won't be confused with the most gracious or forgiving person to ever walk the face of the earth.

But she brings up a valid point: Who is tending to the forgiveness chart?

Not long ago I was giving a Bible study to a young man who attended one of my churches. For a few months we looked at some of the distinctive Adventist doctrines, and when it was all said and done, I asked him if he had any questions. He thought about it for a few seconds and then worked up his courage to say, "Well, actually, yes..." He was very hesitant, however, so I waited for him to complete the thought, "Yes, actually, I do have a question for you."

When I encouraged him to ask the question, an awkward moment of silence followed. He looked down at the floor and out the window before finally looking back at me and asking, "Well, I wanted to know: How many times can I ask God for forgiveness?"

He is not alone. Millions of people around the world, including Bill Clinton, no doubt, are wondering just how many times God will forgive. They want to know if God's forgiveness is limitless or if it can be exhausted. Many of them carry a tremendous amount of guilt around.

This terrible sense of guilt bothered General Romeo Dallaire for much of his post-military experience. General Dallaire, loosely portrayed in the movie *Hotel Rwanda*, was the Canadian who was appointed the Force Commander for the United Nations Assistance Mission for Rwanda when nearly one million Rwandans were killed in an incredible act of genocide. One million Rwandans were killed because the United Nations, along with the Western World, refused to send reinforcements to that country while this mass slaughtering took place. They, or should I say we, simply looked the other way.

General Dallaire and 260 other U. N. Peacekeepers were the only ones deployed to Rwanda when the country needed help the most. For their efforts, Dallaire and the other U. N. forces were able to save over 20,000 Tutsis from the slaughtering of their Hutu enemies.

In spite of his saving efforts and receiving one of the highest military honors awarded to foreigners by the United States, Dallaire suffered major depression when he returned to Canada. It all stemmed from the guilt of what had taken place in Rwanda while the rest of the world continued eating dinner. His depression came to a climax when he was found under a park bench in Quebec, intoxicated and nearly in a coma because of the alcohol mixing with his prescription anti-depressants. He later admitted that he attempted suicide a number of times. Guilt had nearly caused his death.

So it is with many others. Guilt plagues them every day. One teenage girl wrote a letter to Christian author Josh McDowell, sharing the immense pain and guilt she feels from having had an abortion. She wrote,

> The reason I'm writing this is I'm alone and confused. My boyfriend kept pursuing me for sex...I had sex with him thinking that I owed it to him...Later when I learned I was pregnant he blew up, said to get an abortion, and that it was all my fault. So, to save my parents heartache and to keep Matt, I had an abortion. Now Matt has left me... How can God love me after all I have done? Could you please write back? I'm just so confused. Can God really love and forgive me?[1]

To say this girl is hurting is an understatement. She faces the shame and guilt every day of aborting an innocent child. She will never be able to receive forgiveness from the person whose life she took; can she at least receive it from God?

While some wonder how many times they can ask God to forgive them, others wonder if He will even forgive them at all. Thus, we turn to the verse in the Gospels that Hillary referred to.

The passage is found in Matthew 18. There we read of an interesting question that Peter posed to Christ. Matthew recorded, "Then Peter came to Him and said, 'Lord, how often shall my brother sin against me, and I forgive him?'" (Matthew 18:21). The way Peter framed the question revealed his mindset to begin with. He wasn't approaching the subject from a gracious point of view. He didn't say, "Lord, how many times can I shower my brother with grace and mercy before I realize he's not getting the picture?" Instead, he pretty much asked Jesus, "How many times do I have to put up with my brother's foolishness before I can rake him over the coals?"

Peter, ever the impatient and overconfident one, doesn't even give Christ time to answer the question, however. He quips, "Up to seven times?" In Peter's defense, we should note that this was almost certainly a pretty liberal number in the minds of those who witnessed the event. It has been suggested that the Pharisees in Christ's day taught that one should only forgive a person three times before forgiveness ran out. Thus, Peter probably considered himself to be quite generous in his willingness to forgive; he was actually playing the part of a liberal in his day.

The answer Jesus gave must have blown away His listeners. He responded, "I do not say to you, up to seven times, but up to seventy times seven." Can you hear the collective gasps the audience let out? What a scandalous idea! Some of the people couldn't even count that high, no doubt. Yet Jesus tells His listeners to forgive their brothers 490 times.

Of course, as most people observe, Jesus wasn't implying that we should keep strict count. Unlike Hillary Clinton, He wasn't telling us to keep a careful chart, and as soon as a person commits that 491st sin against us, we are then to cease forgiving him. Jesus was using a little bit of divine hyperbole. The point is not the exact number;

it's the importance of our willingness to be gracious and forgiving. Only a large number could emphasize that important message.

To illustrate this point, Jesus then went on to share a parable in which a servant owes his master a large sum of money. The amount in Jesus' day was ten thousand talents, which would be equivalent to roughly $91 million in our day. (Some have suggested it is even equivalent to billions of dollars, a lot of money for even Bill Gates.) That's no "chump" change.

To put it in even greater perspective, the ancient historian Josephus recorded that the annual tribute for all of Judea, Samaria, and Idumea at that time came to only six hundred talents. Thus, Craig Keener commented, "The poor man owes the king more money than existed in circulation in the whole country at the time!"[2] In fact, he owed more than sixteen times the amount of money in circulation. That the king was willing to lend a mere servant that much money to begin with, though certainly stretched out over a period of time, speaks of the king's kind character to begin with.

The servant promises to make good. He says that he will pay his master back, which hardly seems likely. Paying a $91 million debt back doesn't happen overnight. You have to flip a lot of burgers at McDonald's before you have that kind of money.

The reality is that Christ wanted to show the unlikelihood of paying this tremendous debt back. It would take the average person today approximately 4500 years to pay $91 million back, assuming that every penny he earned was used to pay back his debt. That's over 50 lifetimes!

And so it is with God. We can't pay that kind of debt back. The debt that we have accumulated because of our sins couldn't even be paid back with 50 lifetimes of righteous living, let alone the *one* that belongs to us. It doesn't matter who a person is—a murderer, an adulteress, a glutton, a narcissist—each human being is responsible for taking the life of God's Son, which is worth far more than $91 million. In the words of those MasterCard commercials, He is "priceless."

Jesus' listening audience was gearing up for a doozie, no doubt. Certainly the master is going to lay into his servant and torture him because of his inability to pay the debt back. Surprisingly, however, the master doesn't do that, and it isn't until later that he has the servant tortured. It isn't until the servant throws away the forgiveness that he is handed over to the torturers.

Though subtle, these details reveal an important truth of the Gospel. God is never going to turn people over to hell for the debt they have accumulated, for the sins they have committed. In the end, those who are turned over to hell will be so because they threw away God's forgiveness and mercy. That's why I like to say, just as nobody is saved because of their works, but by belief, so no one is lost because of their works, but by their *unbelief*.

So after the servant's appeals, Jesus told us, "Then the master of that servant was moved with compassion, released him, and forgave him the debt" (Matthew 18:27). The servant could walk away totally free of the $91 million debt that he owed. There was nothing written next to his name in the King's books anymore. He was a forgiven man.

This, and especially the rest of the parable, left a remarkable impression on Jesus' listeners, no doubt. They were geared up to hear a story about an exacting master; one who demanded recompense. But this was not the picture that Jesus set before them. They were blindsided by the amazing compassion and forgiveness of a master who deserved repayment.

The story, of course, is so much more than simply a reflection of a fictional king. It is about The King. And it's about you and me. We owe far more than $91 million, yet Jesus is willing and eager to forgive us the debt that we owe.

We need not wonder, then, how many times we can ask Jesus for forgiveness. Nor should we worry that we have done something so heinous that we are beyond God's forgiveness and mercy. If the king in Jesus' story can wipe out a $91 million debt, certainly God can and will do the same for us. In fact, He does much more.

This is why John wrote in his first epistle, "If we confess our sins, He is faithful and just to forgive us our sins and to cleanse us from all unrighteousness" (1 John 1:9). No one should doubt God's forgiveness. John wrote that He is "faithful" to forgive. We don't have to worry about God having a bad hair day, or whether He woke up on the wrong side of the bed. No matter what, He is faithful in forgiving.

Just recently I was reminded of this when I e-mailed a particular person, confessing how I had wronged him in something I'd done. Although e-mailing someone such a confession isn't the best way of going about it, I had been deeply convicted and wanted to "get it off my chest." Plus, he was traveling extensively, and I didn't know when he'd be back in town. So, I sent the e-mail.

After I clicked the "send" button, there was immediate anxiety. I was worried that a million things would go wrong; that perhaps he would come down hard on me because of my sins, or even worse, maybe not even get the e-mail at all. For days I was in limbo, worrying about what would happen. A week or two literally passed before he responded.

We don't have to be in limbo when it comes to God. We don't have to worry that perhaps He didn't get our e-mail; that maybe the heavenly router rejected our message because it had a virus.

By the way, when that person did finally e-mail me back, it was pretty ambiguous. He wrote that he would think about what I had written and get back to me, which he never did. Although I have seen him numerous times since then, the topic has never come up again. Truthfully, if you were to ask me if he forgave my shortcomings, I would have to say, "I don't know."

But this is not the case with Jesus. There is no ambiguity with Him. John told us that He is "faithful" to forgive us. God's faithfulness in forgiving is something we can be assured of. It's one of the constants in life.

More than that, however, John tells us that He is actually "just" to forgive. This seems a bit backwards to us. How is it "just" to forgive someone of such a debt? If a person who committed a tremendous crime were acquitted and forgiven in a court of law, we would cry out that an incredible "injustice" had occurred. We certainly wouldn't think it was "just."

But it is "just" because of who God is. God's government and laws are the opposite of the way we do things; to not forgive or be gracious would be an injustice in God's courts. Something would be seriously wrong if God didn't forgive a person who sincerely requested it. God would be betraying His own character and therefore carrying out an injustice. This is why John could write that God is not only "faithful" in forgiving, but He is also "just."

Yet the beauty of God's forgiveness reaches even further than this. The book of Luke is the only Gospel that recorded one of Jesus' most incredible pleas from the agony of the cross. As the soldiers cast lots to gain the right to take home His garments, Jesus cried out, "Father, forgive them, for they know not what they do" (Luke 23:34, KJV).

As far as I can tell, not one of those soldiers had asked for Jesus' forgiveness, much less His Father's. Yet in the midst of His pain and agony, Jesus declared His unconditional forgiveness and love for those soldiers. He forgave them without their permission or even request.

One can't help thinking of Stephen's last words as he knelt on the ground in the shadows of those who were stoning him. Acts 7:60 tells us that "he knelt down and cried out with a loud voice, 'Lord, do not charge them with this sin.'"

I've always been blown away by Stephen's request. Here was a man who had forgiven his own murderers, as they were in the very *act* of killing him. There was not one bit of remorse on their minds. Yet Stephen didn't let that affect his attitude and forgiveness toward them. In reality, he was merely passing on the unconditional forgiveness that he had received from God.

And so it is with us. Do you realize that you are forgiven in Christ? Do you understand that God's attitude and forgiving heart is present even before we know or request such a thing? Amazingly, Christ forgives us even before we ask Him. It's not as if, when we ask for that forgiveness, Jesus all of a sudden has a change of heart toward us and says, "Oh, yeah...that's a good idea. I guess I'll forgive you if you're going to put it *that* way."

Taking it a step further, if Christ is ever forgiving, it would stand to reason that He has even forgiven those sins that we haven't even committed yet. These things aren't an afterthought to God. We don't have to wake up in the morning worried that He won't forgive us. Just as Christ cried out with a loud voice, "Forgive them" in reference to the soldiers that were nailing Him to the cross, He said that about the entire human race. For we, too, were there that day, driving the nails into His hands.

Five-year-old Kai Leigh Harriott made headlines in Boston, as well as the rest of the United States, in 2006. Kai, who lived in Dorchester—one of the toughest neighborhoods in Boston—suffered perhaps the most tragic accident any person, let alone a child, could endure. The circumstances surrounding the incident weren't normal, either.

On a cool summer night in 2003, Kai and one of her sisters innocently sat on their family's third-story porch, singing "Down by the Bay" from the "Barney" television show. Unbeknownst to the girls, a man was carrying out an argument with two women who lived on the first floor. Trying to scare the women, he fired three gunshots into the air. One of the bullets hit three-year-old Kai, severing her spine. She will be paralyzed for the rest of her life.

Almost three years later, Kai faced, in court, the man who had changed her life forever. He was there to suffer the consequences of his actions, however unintentional they were. After pleading guilty to avoid a trial, and receiving a 13 to 15 year prison sentence, his innocent victim was given the opportunity to address him. With tears in her eyes and amidst an intensely hushed crowd, five-year-old

Kai said, "What you done to me was wrong," and then she softly continued, "But I still forgive him."[3]

The young girl's incredible act of forgiveness amazed everyone. It was the buzz of the city. How a young girl like that, who was banished to a wheelchair for the rest of her life, is able to do such a thing is beyond human comprehension.

Yet it is not beyond divine comprehension. The small girl is but a faint reflection of the Savior's big heart. Facing His perpetrators, Jesus couldn't help saying, "Forgive them." He said that of the Roman soldiers; He says that of us.

What's more, when the trial was over, Kai's mother asked the court officers if she could shake the hand of the man who had paralyzed her daughter. They granted her request, and she approached the man and shook his hand. And then she hugged him. Not only was Kai eager to forgive, but her mother was just as eager to embrace the man who had wronged her daughter.

How much more is Christ willing to do so!

We, too, have been graciously pardoned. We, too, though guilty of the most heinous crime the universe has ever seen—the death of the Son of God—have been "justly" forgiven. Through this act of mercy, Christ hugged and embraced the whole world on Calvary, forgiving each and every person that has ever existed on this planet.

All this, without even the slightest request coming from our lips.

NOTES

1. Josh McDowell and Dick Day, *Why Wait?* (San Bernadino, Calif.: Here's Life Publishers, 1987), 17.

2. Craig S. Keener, *Matthew*. IVP New Testament Commentary (Downers Grove, Ill.: InterVarsity, 1997), 291.

3. Jonathan Saltzman, "'I still forgive him,'" *The Boston Globe*, 14 April 2006, A1?.

SECTION THREE

THE RESPONSIVE BRIDE

CHAPTER XIII

AND THE BRIDE WORE NOTHING

Dear Abby: I am twenty-seven and getting married in September to a wonderful young lady named Julie. She and I are nudists, as is her whole family. We have always wanted an outdoor wedding, and want to have the ceremony at the nudist camp where we met three years ago.

So far, all our invitations have been accepted—except one. You guessed it—the reluctant one is my mother. The non-nudists understand that they will not be required to be nude. My twenty-three-year-old sister and I have tried unsuccessfully to persuade Mother to attend. She refuses to budge, saying if we want her to attend, we will have to change our plans.

Shall we give her an ultimatum and stick with what we want? At this point, I feel like telling my mother we will miss her. What do you say?

Bobby in Nashville[1]

And such is the plight that one young man found himself in. He was greatly torn over the issue of having his wedding in the buff, or having his mother attend.

Quite frankly, I've never heard of a bride who wanted to show up to her wedding naked, have you? Imagine the shock of sitting in the audience at such a wedding and seeing the bride walk down the aisle with nothing on. Many parents would be reaching to cover their children's eyes.

While we can laugh at the situation, the story hits closer to home than we may realize. Could it be that Christ's grand and glorious wedding is also at an impasse because He is dealing with a naked bride too—He also has a bride who wants to march down the aisle with nothing on?

So far we've looked at some important issues in this book. In the first section we saw that Christ's second coming has been delayed because His bride—the Church—has not yet made herself ready. One of the biggest reasons for this is because she has not opened the door to her Lover, who continues to stand at the doorstep, knocking. In the second section we looked at the Bridegroom's beauty. This has hopefully compelled us to open the door to Him, even if just a little.

In this third and final section, we will now turn our attention to the bride. We'll discuss what it means that she is not ready and what she can do, by faith, to ready herself for that glorious wedding, thus hastening Christ's second coming. In many senses, this final section is really the climax of the book, which we've been working up to all along.

As noted in a previous chapter, Revelation 19:7 portrays the beautiful imagery of Christ's wedding finally taking place. After thousands of years of waiting, the great multitude in heaven can finally proclaim, "Let us be glad and rejoice, and give Him glory, for the marriage of the Lamb has come, and His wife has made herself ready." A prepared bride will be what determines when the wedding takes place.

But what does it mean to have a "prepared" bride?

In current times, a million things go into wedding preparations. For months, and sometimes even years, the bride and her family (and many times the groom) will make sure that everything is in place. Flowers have to be ordered; churches have to be reserved; cakes have to be made; ministers have to be consulted; not one thing can be overlooked.

Yet as long as the list is, there is one thing that is most important and that every bride dreams of. While other things may be overlooked and completely forgotten, no bride ever wakes up on the morning of her wedding and says, "Oh, no; I forgot to buy a wedding dress!" I've never heard of such an ordeal. The dress is one of the first things that are procured.

Not surprisingly, this is the very same thing that the book of Revelation focuses on. Even in Biblical times, the bride's attire was what was most important. Thus, after rejoicing that the bride has prepared herself, the multitude signifies that it is because "to her it was granted to be arrayed in fine linen, clean and bright" (Revelation 19:8). This fine linen, to be sure, is the wedding dress.

The message is clear. All the other aspects of wedding preparation mean nothing if the bride doesn't have her wedding dress on. She can have the biggest church, the best programming, the most efficient organizational structure; she can even have a terrific menu planned for the reception—complete with wonderful food that corresponds with the "health message"—but none of it matters if she isn't wearing the wedding dress. God isn't going to get married to a naked bride. Not only would it be embarrassing to the bride, but it would be embarrassing to Him.

This is why the Bible places great emphasis on the matter of nakedness. Throughout scripture we see this being addressed. It's not a coincidence, for example, that one of the first things Adam and Eve notice after they sin is the fact that they are naked. Their nakedness profoundly represented the unrighteousness they had just entered into. To be naked is one of the most shameful states to be in, according to the Bible. Thus, Jesus declares elsewhere in Revelation, "Behold, I am coming as a thief. Blessed is he who watches, and keeps his garments, lest he walk around naked and they see his shame" (Revelation 16:15).

I used to have a roommate in high school who walked around naked fairly regularly. He was known for it. But even more than just walking around our room naked, he would often stand in front of our window and wave to cars driving by. It was a busy street too. What should have been an embarrassing situation, he actually considered entertaining. Sadly, based on Revelation 19:8, I can only conclude that Christ's bride is naked and unashamed as well. Or, perhaps she just doesn't realize her nakedness yet.

This seems to be the message that is presented to the Laodicean church in Revelation 3. Jesus, who is ever the consummate Gentleman, said to the angel of the church of Laodicea, "Because you say, 'I am rich, have become wealthy, and have need of nothing'—and do not realize that you are wretched, miserable, poor, blind, and naked—

I counsel you to buy from Me... white garments, that you may be clothed, that the shame of your nakedness may not be revealed" (Revelation 3:17, 18).

Incidentally, the problem of nakedness is the exact same reason that the Shulamite in the Song of Solomon refused to open the door to her lover. When her lover came and knocked on her door, the Shulamite replied, "I have taken off my robe; how can I put it on again?" (Song of Solomon 5:3). Of course, the difference between the Shulamite and the Laodicean church is that one was aware of her nakedness, while the other wasn't.

But the message to the Laodicean church is pointed and direct. It's not pleasant to talk with someone who is critical of your behavior, especially when you think that everything is just fine. We often like to hear warm fuzzy sermons that tell us everything is all right, that we're doing a good job. It's not politically correct these days to be critical. We promote positive reinforcement, rather than pointing out people's mistakes.

But this is the route that Jesus takes in His message to Laodicea. He doesn't mince any words. He lays it all out there. This is especially reinforced when we remember the beloved's behavior in the Song of Solomon. He didn't simply give the Shulamite's door a love tap; the Hebrew indicated that he banged on the door profusely. Thus, when Christ announces that he stands "at the door and knocks," He's not giving it a gentle love tap either. He's banging on it with all His might. After all, He's trying to wake up His sleeping church. A gentle love tap won't suffice.

This may not correlate with the imagery that is usually painted in relation to the message to Laodicea. We like the idea of Christ standing outside our door with flowers in His hand, asking us, in a "still, small voice," to open to Him. This is no way to approach a person whose house is burning down, however. Something drastic needs to be done. The occupants of the house need to be warned.

We may not like this idea. It may seem harsh to us. Where's the Gospel in such a presentation? How can critical remarks be viewed as loving? Far from being unloving, Christ's message to His bride is extremely loving. To simply let her walk around naked without giving her a warning is altogether uncaring. It's not merciful at all.

Imagine that one day you were going to be given an award at halftime of the Superbowl. Not only would you be able to watch the world's most popular annual event firsthand, but you were going to stand in front of 75,000 people—not to mention 30 million other television viewers—and receive the award.

The day finally comes. You wake up nice and early in the morning, take a shower, put your clothes on, eat breakfast—complete with Morning Star breakfast links, of course—and drive to the stadium. When you arrive at the stadium, you are escorted to a room to wait there until halftime. You're nervous as you wait, but then the moment finally arrives. Two men come and lead you out to the field.

As you make your way to the field, you pass a few people. They look at you and smile, congratulate you, and continue on their merry way. Then you see a few of your family members. They look at you and smile and wish you good luck. Then you notice that the two security guards who are escorting you out to the field have a kind of smirk on their faces as well. Perplexed by their curious grins, you nonetheless shrug it off and continue out to the field.

You finally make it to the middle of the field where you'll be presented with the award. The award presenter greets you, and his face also breaks out with a little smirk. By this time you're a little curious. Then 75,000 people turn their collective attention to you, and as you're being presented with the award, you suddenly realize that the whole stadium is laughing hysterically at you.

You break out in a cold sweat. *What is wrong with these people?* you wonder. And then, just as the laughter has reached its climax, you look up at the giant jumbo-tron and realize that your worst nightmare has come true: your zipper is down.

How embarrassing would that be? What's worse, what happened to all the people that saw you before you took center stage? Even your family saw your situation and didn't point it out to you. It certainly would have been nice of them to let you in on the joke before you were exposed to the whole world.

Yet they didn't say anything because they didn't want to be critical; they didn't want to step on your toes. They just wanted to affirm you and make it sound as if everything was all right.

But their actions certainly weren't loving at all. The loving action would have been to critically inform you of your state.

This is the situation that Christ finds Himself in. He just can't sit back and let His bride walk around naked. He must warn her. He wants to save His lovely bride the embarrassment of standing before the universe in her birthday suit. His critical warning to Laodicea is the most loving thing He can do.

While we may view the illustration as somewhat funny, it is a very serious matter. The implication of the bride's nakedness stretches far and wide. Because the bride has yet to put the wedding dress on, time has been allowed to linger far too long. Don't get me wrong; we should ever be eager to delay the Lord's coming, in some senses, so that we can bring more people to Christ. But the greatest single thing the church can do to win more souls to Christ is to put on the wedding dress once and for all. This would be the greatest evangelistic tool ever invented. Those whom Jesus has been patiently waiting for all this time would finally surrender to Him.

But this will only take place when the church is clothed in that wedding dress. Until then, time continues. And millions of people die worldwide.

I realized the seriousness of this matter recently when the United States was hit with its worst natural disaster, Hurricane Katrina. Through this single catastrophe, thousands of people died, not to mention the millions upon millions of dollars' worth of destruction that devastated the Gulf states.

The epiphany came, however, when I realized that I, in a profound way, was responsible for this disaster. No,

I wasn't responsible for the mighty winds that swept through the Gulf states. It wasn't my personal fault that the infrastructure of New Orleans was so weak that the whole city virtually collapsed. Rather, because of my personal refusal to put on that wedding dress, I have delayed Christ's return, thus allowing disaster after disaster to rock this world.

The responsibility doesn't rest solely on me, of course, nor does it rest solely on you. The book of Revelation tells us that only when the whole church puts on the wedding dress corporately does the wedding finally take place. No individual person is responsible for single-handedly causing this to take place, but each of us can certainly make a difference.

As I mentioned in a previous chapter, I realize this may come as a shock to you and perhaps even seem heretical. But I'd like you to take a moment and honestly ask yourself this ever-important question: Why hasn't Christ returned yet? I think this is the single biggest question that God's people need to ask. Never mind questions about women's ordination, or worship styles, or eating cheese. While I understand that all these things have their place, they are only important as they fit into the context of hastening Christ's Second Coming.

Though some people may simply diminish the question by saying God has reasons that are unknown to us, I believe the Bible plainly gives the reason. As we have seen, Revelation 19 says that the marriage of the Lamb will come when His "bride has made herself ready" by being "arrayed in fine linen, clean and bright."

But because the bride has wanted to remain naked for too long, the world suffers.

The implications are frightening.

If the bride had put on the wedding dress when Christ initially wanted her to, we wouldn't have had the bloodiest century the world has ever experienced. Six million Jews wouldn't have been killed. Acts of genocide in Yugoslavia, Rwanda, and Sudan wouldn't have taken place, not to mention civil war in dozens of other countries. September

11 wouldn't have occurred. Hurricane Katrina could have been avoided.

Instead, because of our refusal to put on that wedding dress, we have caused more pain in the heart of God through these events than He ever should have experienced. It's no wonder that Christ eagerly knocks on Laodicea's door and says, "I counsel to you to buy from Me...white garments, that you may be clothed" (Revelation 3:18).

He's inviting us to do the same. As individuals. As a church.

NOTES

1. Abigail Van Buren, *Dear Abby on Planning Your Wedding* (Kansas City, Mo.: Andrews and McMeel, c1988), 13, 14.

CHAPTER XIV

GOD'S MASTERPIECE

There's probably nothing more annoying than going to a wedding where the formal pictures are taken between the wedding and the reception. I recently heard of a couple that took four hours to get to the reception site after the wedding was over because they were taking their pictures. These days, most couples take pictures before the wedding, thus sparing their guests any significant wait.

But I was one of those annoying people. Although we took some of our formal pictures before the wedding—with our groomsmen and bridesmaids—I demanded that the bride-and-groom pictures be taken after the wedding. I'll be honest with you; I'm a sentimental guy, and I wanted to do the old traditional routine where the groom doesn't see the bride until she's marching down the aisle.

Part of the reason was because of the wedding dress. I didn't want to see it before the ceremony. I figured that I had not been allowed to see it for the five or six months before our wedding, so why would I want to spoil the surprise by seeing it 30 minutes before the event? It's like opening your Christmas presents on Christmas Eve. Some people do this, I know, but it's just not right, in my opinion.

The wedding dress, of course, is one of the most important elements of the wedding. It's probably right up there with the bride and groom as to what's most important. Girls dream about what their wedding dress will look like from a very young age. Some even dress up in them and pretend they are getting married when they're little girls.

I can remember when my wife started looking for her wedding dress. Although she probably wasn't one of those girls who had fantasized about her dress as a young girl, it was still exciting for her, nonetheless. And after searching for a dress that matched her taste and her budget, she finally settled on one.

I wasn't allowed to see it, of course, and the next few months were spent trying to transport it without letting me catch a glimpse of it. Many other people were allowed to see it, but they were sworn to secrecy as to what it looked like. Camille certainly wouldn't give me any hints as to its appearance. The only thing she assured me of was that it was white. I was greatly relieved to hear this. What a nightmare it would have been to see her marching down the aisle in a black or pink or turquoise dress!

Unlike much of society, I still believe that the wedding dress signifies something. There was a time when most people would have agreed with this idea. If a woman wore a white dress, she was wearing it for a reason. It meant that she was pure and was truly giving herself fully to the man who was to be her husband. In essence, what the dress looked like—both design and color—were indicative of who the woman was. It was a window into her character.

In the last chapter we noted that Christ's bride will finally be ready when she puts on the wedding dress. But what does this mean? What is so significant about the wedding dress? Is it also indicative of the bride's character?

Fortunately, the book of Revelation doesn't keep us guessing. The same verse we looked at in the last chapter shares insight into this subject. There, we are told a few important details of what the bride's wedding dress is all about.

As we noted in the last chapter, the great multitude in Revelation 19 are excited because the marriage of the Lamb is finally going to take place. All the preparations are over, and they shout out, "Let us be glad and rejoice and give Him glory, for the marriage of the Lamb has come, and His wife has made herself ready" (Revelation 19:7). They then go on to signify what has finally made the bride ready. They say in the next verse, "And to her it was granted to be arrayed in fine linen, clean and bright."

Notice the very first element of the bride's attire. The multitude says that "to her it was *granted* to be arrayed in fine linen." A more literal translation for the word "granted" would be that she was "given" the wedding dress. In other words, it is free. She hasn't purchased it with her own money. Somebody graciously gave it to her.

You probably appreciate the significance of this idea if you have been married or are in the process of planning the event. Wedding dresses aren't usually free. They aren't thrown in as an extra bonus for renting a church hall. There are no, "Been there, done that, got the free wedding dress" bumper stickers that I've seen. Wedding dresses are usually one of the most expensive parts of the wedding.

The price of my wife's dress was nearly 10% of the total budget for our wedding. This, for a dress that has been sitting in our closet since our wedding day, which she will probably wear twice in her life—once in public on her wedding day, and the other in the privacy of our own room as she tries to fit into it after 30 years.

The words in Revelation remind me all too vividly of the parable Jesus told in Matthew 22. We're all familiar with the story, I'm sure. A certain king had a son who was having a wedding, so the king invited all his friends to come and celebrate. Unfortunately, they were all busy, so the king had his servants go into the highways and invite everyone they could to the wedding. They came in droves. When the king came in to see his guests, however, he noticed that one man who had entered didn't have a wedding garment on. The king wondered, "Friend, how did you come in here without a wedding garment?" (Matthew 22:12). Jesus tells us that the man was "speechless." He had no answer for the king; not even an acknowledgment of his wrongdoing.

The story doesn't end gloriously. The king tells his servants to bind the man and cast him into outer darkness. How unfortunate! The king was eager to place a wedding garment on the man. Everyone who entered into the wedding was given one. But this man refused the free gift.

So it is in these last days. Christ's greatest desire is to place that wedding dress on each one of us so that He will have a prepared bride. Will we reject that free gift that He gives to us? It would be well to remember those words in

Revelation 16:15, "Blessed is he who watches, and keeps his garments, lest he walk around naked and they see his shame."

It must be pointed out, though, that just because the wedding dress that God places on His bride is free, that doesn't mean it didn't cost anything. It's free for the recipient; but, just as with any gift that is given, it cost the Giver a great amount of money. In fact, our Savior paid an infinite price in securing that wedding dress for us: He gave His blood, which is far more costly than anything the world can produce. Indeed, as we noticed in the Song of Solomon, Christ gave "all the wealth of His house for love" (Song of Songs 8:7).

Revelation's description of the bride's wedding dress continues. Not only is the dress freely given to the bride, but we read that it is "clean and bright." We would expect this, of course. I've never seen a bride who wore a dirty dress to her wedding. The dress hardly leaves the confines of the bride's closet in the months leading up to the wedding. She wants to make sure that nothing happens to it, that it remains pure and beautiful for the big day.

What's more, I would have certainly wondered about my bride if she had walked down the aisle with big splotches of mud on her dress. Not only would it have been embarrassing for her, but I would have been very embarrassed as well. And, with all sincerity, it would have definitely made me question her love for me. If she didn't care enough to make sure her dress was clean, how could I expect her to care for me?

Fortunately, my beautiful bride did have a clean dress on. And all eyes were on her as she marched down the aisle with her dad.

Some of us have the impression that God is going to simply put our wedding dress in a giant washing machine every time we sin and clean our dress until eternity. One of my good friends, with whom I was in a musical group in college, wrote a clever little song called "The Jeans Song" that spoke somewhat about this subject. It was a very catchy song in which the chorus said,

So scrub me up, bleach me out
Show me what grace is all about
Put my dirty laundry into Your machine
With the tide of Your blood
Wisk away my sin and mud
And don't stop washing me until I am clean

Don't get me wrong; the song is completely full of the Gospel and rightfully explains Christ's forgiveness. The beauty of the Gospel says that Christ does and will cleanse us whenever we dirty ourselves. He picks us up whenever we fall. There can be no doubting this.

But the even greater truth of the Gospel—and I know that my friend understands this—is that Christ desires still so much more for us. He'd like to teach us, by His grace, to avoid dirtying our dress in the first place. As Jude 24 says, "Now to Him who is able to keep you from stumbling..." At some point the bride has to show up to the wedding with a completely clean dress on. It won't suffice for her to fall down in the mud on the way to the wedding.

We'll look at this a little more in-depth in a few chapters, but until then, we can rest assured that Christ's greatest desire is that His bride allow Him to help her completely overcome by His grace.

This is why Revelation 19:8 clarifies this thought. The verse continues by saying, "For the fine linen is the righteous acts of the saints." The verse doesn't say that the fine linen is the "righteous acts" of Christ. This is not to say that the bride is in any way responsible for these righteous acts apart from Christ. But the point is made that this righteousness truly becomes a part of who the bride is; it represents the character that she has allowed Christ to weave into her life.

What this verse has described is the essence of "Righteousness by Faith." I'm sure you've heard this phrase before; we talk a lot about it as Adventists. It seems to be one of those buzz phrases that many people talk about. Some people understand it, but even fewer implement it into their lives.

Notice the characteristics of what righteousness by faith is according to this verse. We see, first of all, that it is a gift from God. Thus, we read in Isaiah 61:10, "For He has clothed me with the garments of salvation, He has covered me with the robe of righteousness." The verse goes on to compare this to a bride that "adorns herself with her jewels."

Indeed, the dress that the bride will wear will shine brightly forth as Christ's gift of righteousness. Left to ourselves, we would wear nothing but filthy rags. That is why I love the imagery set forth in the book of Zechariah. There we read the story of a High Priest named Joshua who stands before the Angel of the Lord. Satan is there accusing Joshua because he is "clothed with filthy garments." God responds by saying, "Take away the filthy garments from him," and then says, "See, I have removed your iniquity from you, and I will clothe you with rich robes" (Zechariah 3:4).

We can all be thankful that God doesn't allow us to continue wearing our filthy garments. Neither does He allow us to be naked. Instead, He takes the filthy garments off and places His righteousness on us. We are then arrayed in the most fashionable clothing the universe has ever seen. Any Hollywood star would be envious of this wedding dress.

But some people stop there. They often confuse righteousness by faith with forgiveness by faith. For them, Christ secures our salvation by placing this robe of righteousness on us, but that is the extent of the power of Christ's grace. Underneath this robe we are still unrighteous.

While it is true that Christ's righteousness always covers up our deficiencies, as we noted before, this robe of righteousness also becomes a part of who we are. It is woven into our characters so that we can become like Christ. This is the essence of righteousness by faith. It is living righteously by faith.

This righteous living, of course, is *never* the basis for our salvation; it is simply the natural result of it. When people come to an appreciation for what Christ has done for them, they naturally want to live for Him. This is why Paul wrote, "For the love of Christ compels us, because we judge thus: that if One died for all, then all died; and He died for all, that those who live should no longer live for themselves, but for Him who died for them and rose again" (2 Corinthians 5:14, 15).

The *agape* love of Christ—that which is seen most clearly on the cross—compels us to live for Him. We want to return our lives back to Him out of appreciation for His sacrifice on the cross. Thus, a few verses later Paul again wrote, "For He made in Him who knew no sin to be sin for us, that we might become the righteousness of God in Him" (2 Corinthians 5:21). Elsewhere, we see Paul again wrote, "For by grace you have been saved through faith, and that not of yourselves; it is the gift of God, not of works, lest anyone should boast. For we are His workmanship, created in Christ Jesus for good works" (Ephesians 2:8-10).

Not only did Christ die for us so that we might be justified, but He also died for us so that we would be "His workmanship, created in Christ Jesus for good works." The word used for "workmanship" in Greek is "*poiema*," from which we get our English word "poem." It is that which is created or made. One version translates this word as "masterpiece."

I love that idea. We are God's poem. We are His masterpiece that He has intricately composed, His magnum opus that He has written. Of all the places in the universe God has created, we are, for some reason, the greatest song or piece of literature He has ever written.

Have you ever been to the symphony? Perhaps you don't like classical music, and I understand. But maybe you can apply this analogy to whatever type of music you do enjoy listening to. When we hear a beautiful song, our hearts are naturally turned towards the composer of that song, especially if it is beautiful. While we may marvel at those who perform the song, we are really impressed with the person who created it, particularly if it's Mozart or Beethoven, who were deaf when they composed much of their music.

This is the beauty of what God wants to do through us. He wants to bless the universe with His beautiful masterpiece—us. In turn, we, too, are definitely blessed to be a part of that masterpiece, to know that we can be the crowning achievement in God's creative accomplishments.

The truth of the matter is that Christ didn't die so that we would be on a life-support system for the rest of our lives here on earth. He didn't die so that we would be an out-of-tune note on the pages of His score. Christ died so that we might "have life" and have it "more abundantly" (John 10:10).

This is what righteousness by faith is all about. It's about returning to the pages of God's Masterpiece and allowing our lives to gloriously and harmoniously bring honor and glory to the Author of that masterpiece. This is what can happen when the bride allows Christ to place that robe of righteousness on her.

But it can't be done by individuals. A masterpiece entails many different notes. One note doesn't make a song. So, although we as individuals may be in tune, God will not be glorified until His entire church—His bride—ultimately falls into harmony with each other and with Him.

Then, the greatest symphony the universe has ever witnessed will be played and enjoyed. The universe will naturally want to sing in response, and they will collectively shout out with a loud voice, "Worthy is the Lamb who was slain to receive power and riches and wisdom, and strength and honor and glory and blessing!" (Revelation 5:12).

CHAPTER XV

WHAT DOEST THOU FOR ME?

I'd like you to close your eyes for a second. Wait a minute, open them up again. You won't be able to read this if your eyes are closed. So just imagine with me, if you will.

Imagine that the day has finally come. You see that dark cloud coming from the east that gets bigger and bigger. Pretty soon the whole world has turned its collective attention to it. Graves are turned open, and the dead start floating up to meet God in the air. You soon join them as all of God's people make their way to heaven.

After a long trip you finally see those pearly gates that you have heard so much about. As you approach, you notice a curious looking gentleman sitting at the entrance. Thinking it is St. Peter, you soon realize he is walking alongside you because this is his first visit to the Holy City as well. Upon further inspection, you soon realize it is Moses, who has been waiting for this grand and glorious day for thousands of years.

He greets us and makes small talk, and then motions us through the gates and says, "Enjoy your stay. Let us know if we can do anything to make it more enjoyable for you." So with great anticipation and joy, you walk through those humungous pearly gates. You're enamored by their beauty and majesty.

And then, as you walk into paradise, you look and see a startling scene. It almost knocks you over like a bolt of lightning as you stand in shock and disbelief. There, before you, stretching infinitely across the heavenly horizon is a gigantic desert of nothingness, complete with tumbleweed that rolls across the parched and arid landscape.

Of course, you're confused. So you look closer. And then you notice hundreds of feet away a small, little shack with a sputtering neon sign on the top that says, "New Jerusalem." *What?* you wonder, *This is the New Jerusalem?* You just can't comprehend what you're seeing. You think maybe you took the wrong bus, or got off at the

wrong stop. Maybe this is hell rather than heaven. It sure
seems like it.

Frantic, you return to Moses and ask him where you
are. He assures you that it's heaven; this is where you
will spend the next thousand years. There are no streets
of gold, no big mansions, no sea of glass to walk on, no
giraffes whose necks you can slide down; there's not even
a Taco Bell within 30 million miles.

So what would you do? Would you ask for a return
ticket back to earth?

The picture that I just had you imagine is quite silly, I
know, *and there is not one bit of truth to it*. I once painted
this scenario for a group of kids that I was talking with,
and some of them were quite disturbed. Immediately after
I finished the talk, I had two teenage girls—probably 16
or 17—come up to me and tell me how upset they were
at me. Apparently, they couldn't get past what I had said.
They didn't hear the rest of the talk because they were
so hung up on the picture I had painted in their minds.
Nothing I could say alleviated their concerns, and they
ended up criticizing everything I said the whole weekend I
was there speaking.

I can assure you that heaven is nothing like the picture
I just had you imagine. It is the most beautiful place in
the universe. The Bible is very clear on this. There will,
indeed, be streets of gold and big mansions and giraffes,
to boot.

But I wanted to paint this scenario in your mind to
get you to think. What *if* heaven were a dry, ugly place?
Would you still want to go there? What's more, would the
Christian life still be worth living if we had no promise of
eternal life at all? What if this life were all that we had?

I'd like to pause in this chapter for a brief moment to look
at these ideas. After discussing the ideas of righteousness
by faith in the previous chapter, I think a lot of it boils
down to motivation—what motivates a person to act the
way they do. Sadly, many people are simply serving God
out of fear or the hope of a future reward. Their motivation
stems nothing from a deep appreciation for what God has

done for them. I think we, as Christians, need to move beyond this, and we need to truly live by faith.

The word "faith" is one of the most misunderstood words in the English language. Although it's perhaps the most fundamental aspect of the Christian experience, many people are at a loss to explain or understand what faith truly is.

So what is it? Have you ever thought about it before? I think many of us take it for granted. We've heard for so long that we need to "live by faith" but, in the end, we're not really sure what that means. How does a person *live* by faith, anyway? And more specifically, how does a person live *righteously* by faith?

The significance of these questions cannot be emphasized enough. In the book of Romans, Paul wrote that "whatever is not from faith is sin" (Romans 14:23). That is a serious statement. What Paul says is that no matter what we do, if we're not doing it by faith then we are sinning. This kind of makes things sticky. Mere outward actions can't reveal, in the end, whether a person is sinning or not. I can be going to church every Sabbath, paying a regular tithe, not wearing jewelry, eating my Special K loaf, yet all the while sinning, if these actions aren't the result of a faith that is implemented in my life.

It tells me, then, that this faith thing is pretty serious. We better get it figured out if we want to prepare ourselves for that great wedding day. After all, Revelation tells us that one of the key characteristics of God's last-day people are those who have "the faith of Jesus" (Revelation 14:12).

So what is it?

One of the first answers to this question, inevitably, is that faith is best defined by "trust." The Bible certainly establishes this idea firmly. Proverbs 3:5, 6, for example, says, "Trust in the Lord with all your heart, and lean not on your own understanding; in all your ways acknowledge Him, and He shall direct your paths." There is much to be said for placing our trust firmly in Christ every day. He does, indeed, provide for our every need. We should be ever mindful of this.

Further solidifying this idea of faith being trust are object lessons, such as the "trust fall." This is where someone falls back and is caught by a group of people who have their arms interlocked. The whole idea is to illustrate how we can trust God, knowing that He'll always catch us. We have nothing to fear.

While faith certainly includes trust, however, it is merely one aspect of it. It doesn't encapsulate the whole of it. Trust can only take a person so far in his or her experience with Christ.

Trust is what a young child does with his parents. He trusts that they will provide for his needs; that they will give him food when he's hungry, or put clothes on his body. It's almost second nature. But a child, until he matures, cannot go any further. While he's putting his simple trust in his parents, he's asking nothing of what he can do for them.

That is the very nature of trust; it is only concerned about its own needs being met. Think of the "trust fall" again. When a person falls back, trusting that his friends will catch him, he is only worried about his own safety. He's not thinking about his friend Bob who might sprain his wrist trying to catch him, or Sue who might be thirsty. That's not his concern at the time. He's only thinking about himself.

This is the extent of many people's faith-experience. They are babes in Christ and have not yet matured enough to move beyond simply focusing on their own needs. And that's fine. Everyone is at a different place in his or her walk with God. It would be unfair to expect people to run before they can even crawl.

I don't want to downplay this aspect of faith at all. Nowadays, many people struggle with trust. Whereas a hundred years ago everyone in society could be trusted, we're now told no one can be, even our own family members. A lot of this is the result of battered and torn families. People who come from homes where their parents are divorced are challenged by trusting people.

Trust has never been an issue for me, personally. I come from a very healthy family situation. For this reason, I don't want to brush aside this aspect of faith simply because I'm not challenged by it. My wife, on the other hand, comes from a family with divorced parents. Trusting others doesn't come as easily to her. There were definite questions of trust in her mind when we started dating and when we were talking about marriage.

Thus, learning how to trust God can be a huge hurdle for many people. Coming to the place where they feel confident that the Lord will provide for their needs— whether spiritual or temporal—may take some time.

The point is, however, that we shouldn't limit our faith to this. Trust is just one tiny aspect of faith. And some of us can't get past it; we have been walking with God for a long time without seeing any type of maturation. We are crippled in many ways and unable to ask God about how we can help Him. Our eyes have been resting solely on ourselves.

I can't help thinking of an experience that the disciples shared with Jesus on a stormy Galilean boat excursion. The winds started swirling, and the waves started crashing. The disciples feared for their lives while Jesus slept peacefully in the stern of the boat. With great terror the disciples shouted out with one accord, "Lord, save us! We are perishing!" (Matthew 8:25).

Although Jesus ultimately calmed the storm, He was greatly hurt by His disciples and asked, "Why are you fearful, O you of little faith?" The disciples' terror revealed their lack of faith. To be sure, Jesus was disappointed that they didn't feel confident that He would keep them safe, but look again at their statement. The disciples blurted out, "Lord, save *us*! *We* are perishing!" None of them seemed the slightest bit concerned that their Savior was sleeping quietly on the floor of the boat as the ship was sinking. Not one of them ran over to Him and said, "Hey, uh, Jesus, You might want to wake up because the ship is going down. We don't want You to be sleeping with the fishes in a few seconds." They had no concern for the fact that, perhaps, He could perish. Instead, they were only concerned about their own safety and well-being.

Surely, this can't be the model of a healthy and vibrant faith. This can't be the type of faith that is talked about when speaking of righteousness by faith either. This type of faith seems to focus only on self; whereas, true righteous living, by its very definition, focuses on other people's needs.

One of the most helpful passages in the Bible that I find enlightens my ideas on faith is found in Galatians 5:6. There, Paul wrote, "For in Christ Jesus neither circumcision nor uncircumcision avails anything." Paul seems to be saying the same thing we looked at before. In our contemporary context, it's almost as if he is saying, "Keeping the Sabbath or not keeping the Sabbath isn't going to get you any brownie points. It's not going to get you into heaven." He goes on to say, however, that what matters most is "faith working through love."

According to Paul, what matters most is faith manifesting itself through love. In my mind, this seems to be the clearest and most practical explanation as to how faith works. It's not some abstract concept or selfish "me-first" attitude. Love is the true expression of faith.

Faith, in essence, is the heart's response to God's love and initiative. Some people have described it as saying "yes" to God. Abraham certainly exercised this in the book of Genesis when God promised Him a son. Genesis tells us, in response to God's promise, that Abraham "believed in the Lord, and He accounted it to him for righteousness" (Genesis 15:6). The literal Hebrew of the passage indicates that Abraham said "Amen!" to God. He was overwhelmed with joy upon hearing God's wonderful promises. His heart, in some senses, skipped a beat. It jumped for joy.

This is why, as we noted in the last chapter, Paul wrote elsewhere, "For the love of Christ compels us, because we judge thus: that if One died for all, then all died" (2 Corinthians 5:14). When people understand and appreciate that which God has done for them, especially as seen on the cross, they are compelled to give their lives back to Him. Thus, they are liberated from a pre-occupation with self and overwhelmed by a tremendous sense of gratitude for Christ.

Thus, Paul wrote that faith expresses itself through love. The heart is compelled by Christ's love and, in turn, expresses itself through love as well. Love, after all, is the epitome of other-centeredness.

I used to tell people that when I got a girlfriend, I would take the term "whipped" to new heights. I would be her slave. If she would say, "Jump!" I would say, "How high?" This is because, in love, I would naturally want to do nice things for her. I would naturally want to make her happy.

No doubt we've all heard the story about the slave that was purchased at an auction, vowing to never work for his master. The whole way home he repeated to the man who had purchased him that he would never work; he was going to be rebellious. When the master and his new slave arrived home, the master took the slave by surprise by releasing him, telling him he was free. Overwhelmed with gratitude, the slave said that he would serve the master for the rest of his life and do anything for him.

This is what faith is all about. It's understanding the tremendous freedom Christ has purchased for us with His blood and returning our lives back to Him.

Thus, selfish desires get lost in the shuffle. Our experience with Christ, and the reason we serve Him, no longer is about simply gaining heaven or escaping hell. We don't serve Him because we want to live forever in a big, nice mansion or have an endless supply of mango juice. We serve Him happily because we have been overwhelmed with a sense of gratitude. We serve Him because we have been compelled by love.

Of course, this is not to say that the life of faith will always be peachy. It would be naïve to say that in every situation we face, we'll have a song in our heart or an overwhelming sense of gratitude that compels us to always do the right thing. I once had a friend who struggled with this idea. A few months after explaining this idea to him, he asked me what was going wrong in his life. He still didn't feel compelled to serve the Lord. The sense of gratitude didn't overwhelm him.

We have to remember that faith is not a feeling. Although there can be feelings involved, if we are simply waiting for this to somehow take control of our bodies, we are perhaps misled. In all honesty, there are times when living our faith is a struggle. We may not *feel* compelled to do that which we know to be right, but God's grace will help us overcome those despondent feelings.

It certainly wouldn't be healthy for us to live the majority of our lives this way, however; to be holding ourselves at gun-point to do the right thing. There should be an underlying peace that defines our lives and actions. This is what David meant when he said, "I delight to do Your will, O my God, and Your law is within my heart" (Psalm 40:8). Ultimately, the life that is resting in Christ is defined by delighting to do His will. It's nothing that has to be forced; it's a faith that naturally grows out of appreciation for Christ's love and grace.

To me, Paul and Moses are the epitome of the life of faith. Both lived out their faith in a way that, in my opinion, was only surpassed by Christ, Himself. After the Israelites danced around the golden calf and God threatened to wipe them out, Moses pleaded, "Yet now, if You will forgive their sin—but if not, I pray, blot me out of Your book which You have written" (Exodus 32:32). Paul wrote in Romans 9:3, "For I could wish that I myself were cursed and cut off from Christ for the sake of my brothers, those of my own race" (NIV).

These two men were so compelled by the love of God that they were willing to forfeit eternal life for the sake of their people. They put other people's interests, as well as God's, ahead of their own. They were responding by faith.

One of the most interesting figures in the 18th century was a man by the name of Count Nikolaus von Zinzendorf. He founded a group known as the Moravian Brethren, located in Germany. The group emphasized a religious experience of the cross and the heart. The great English revivalist John Wesley, in fact, was immensely influenced by their religion of the heart, though he and Zinzendorf had a falling out with each later on.

Zinzendorf himself didn't always have an experience with Christ. He wasn't converted until he was 19. It happened as he was traveling through the capital cities of Europe as a part of his educational requirements. He was in an art gallery in the city of Dusseldorf one day when he became deeply enthralled with one particular painting. It was a painting by Domenico Feti called *Ecce Homo*, that portrayed Christ bloodied and wearing the crown of thorns. The painting was so gripping, and the words underneath cut to Zinzendorf's heart immensely. In bold letters, the words jumped out at him, "All this I did for thee; what doest thou for me?"[1]

The words changed his life forever. They can do the same for us.

Christ stands before us, carrying the sins of the world on His shoulders. He has experienced the full weight of hell's fury. The wrath of God is upon Him. And He looks at us, with tears in His eyes, and wonders, "All this I did for thee; what doest thou for Me?"

We can respond by faith.

NOTES

1. Stott, 294.

CHAPTER XVI

NO MORE DIRTY DISHES

I wash the dishes in our household. My wife and I have had an agreement ever since we have been married; even before, actually. She cooks and I do the dishes. It's an arrangement that has worked out pretty nicely, although it seems like the dishes never stop. They keep piling up. Just when I think I've done them all, it seems as if I have to start all over again.

Have you ever had such an experience?

Suppose that I come home one day and tell my wonderful wife, Camille, that I want to take her out on a date. She would, no doubt, be extremely excited.

But then I tell her there is a catch. I will only take her out *after* all the dishes are done.

So I tell her what I am going to do, and I start out on my task. I'm sure if this were a typical situation, there would be a big pile of dishes already in the sink from a day's worth of eating. So I start washing them, and after I get through a number of dishes, I start to notice something strange. Just like the five loaves and two fishes seemed to never disappear, these dishes seem to be endless as well. Frustrated, I start scrubbing harder and faster. But it doesn't work. And then I start noticing some of the same dishes that I have already washed. But there they are, dirty again, ready to be washed.

And then I finally notice it: my wife has been placing these dishes in the sink all along. So I say to her, "Hey, Toots [that's what I call her], you keep piling more dishes up." To which she responds, "Oh, yeah...sorry. Please forgive me." Forgiving her, I keep washing away, only to notice that she places more dirty dishes in the sink.

At this point I am really frustrated, of course, and get a little more serious in my declarations, "Camille: stop putting dirty dishes in the sink." Her response is the same, however, and she gives me a little smile and a kiss on the cheek and says, "Oh, yeah. You forgive me, don't you?"

I would forgive her, but on and on it goes. She keeps piling dirty dishes upon dirty dishes. She stacks them up to the ceiling, all the while knowing that I will keep good on my promise to wash them all.

The question is: If Camille kept piling the dirty dishes up and I kept washing them, would we *ever* go on our date?

I realize that this scenario is somewhat simplistic and quite unrealistic—especially since Camille would never do such a thing—but it paints a picture, nonetheless. Not only would it seriously delay the timing of our date—and perhaps even cancel it altogether—but it would certainly cause me to question my wife's love to begin with. You see, if she truly loved me, you would think that she would do all that she could to hasten the date. And you would certainly think that she would want to alleviate the amount of stress that I was experiencing by not producing as many dirty dishes.

Yet this is a very real reflection of our present situation. Many people have the impression that Christ's bride will be placing dirty dishes in the sink pretty much until she is on her way to heaven, but I'm not so sure this is what the Bible teaches. I think there's better news for us than that.

The place we see this issue most clearly is in the sanctuary. We briefly discussed the sanctuary in a few previous chapters, but it would be well for us to visit it again. Many Adventists do not fully understand the sanctuary doctrine. Some think that our views on the sanctuary are all about the pre-Advent judgment. God is judging the earth, we have heard people say, and we had better get ready in case our name comes up. After all, we don't want to be sinning when Jesus is reviewing our case.

Still, others have the idea that the sanctuary doctrine simply enlightens our ideas on forgiveness and intercession. Whenever we sin, Jesus pleads our name before the Father, and we are forgiven. It becomes an endless cycle that no human being can ever put behind him.

While both of these ideas contain elements of truth, they lack the full force of what the sanctuary is all about. The sanctuary is much more than simply about judgment or forgiveness. It's about Christ's grace that can teach a person to say "no" to ungodliness.

We see this idea in the book of Leviticus, a book that we don't read very often. If you've ever set forth to read the whole Bible through, you have, no doubt, gotten discouraged when you reached Leviticus, if you even made it through the whole of Exodus. I know I've been discouraged by it before. The book contains chapter after chapter about different rituals and laws, detailed to the minutest points.

But at the heart of Leviticus is the Gospel. Here we see the wonderful truth about the sanctuary.

As we discovered before, the Israelite sanctuary services were set up in a very specific way. Every day throughout the year, the priest would sacrifice different types of animals for all of Israel. Lambs, rams, or doves would be brought before the altar and sacrificed for the people. The blood that these animals shed was to cover the sins of those in the camp. Through this the people were forgiven.

But, although those sins were forgiven, they weren't totally eradicated altogether. The forgiven sins were all placed in the sanctuary itself, much like a dirty dish is placed into a sink. It wasn't until the Day of Atonement, the one day of the year when the High Priest would enter into the Most Holy Place of the sanctuary, that all the "dirty dishes" that had piled up in the sanctuary were totally removed forever. On that one day, forgiveness was not the goal. The goal was total cleansing and removal of sin.

This is what Leviticus 16:30 says, "For on that day the priest shall make atonement for you, to cleanse you, that you may be clean from all your sins before the Lord." It is also the same idea that John emphasizes in his first epistle when he wrote, "If we confess our sins, He is faithful and just to forgive us our sins and to cleanse us from all unrighteousness" (1 John 1:9). It is the essence of the whole sanctuary service. There was, first of all, forgiveness of sins that took place throughout the year, and then there was a cleansing from all unrighteousness that took place on the Day of Atonement.

We, of course, believe that there has been an antitypical Day of Atonement going on since 1844. But what many of us miss is the fact that God's ministry has moved from the Holy Place—where He was solely focused on the ministry of forgiveness for 1800 years after His ascension—into the Most Holy Place. Here He has been working on cleansing people from all their sins.

As Roy Gane puts it,

> By His Spirit, God can speed up the spiritual growth of His people so that they outgrow sin. By cleansing His people and presenting them to Himself without blemish, Christ works Himself out of the job of forgiving sins. He does not walk off the job. We could say that He is "laid off" from this work because there are no more forgivable sins to forgive.[1]

Don't misunderstand me. This isn't to say that forgiveness is not available during this time or that we will be lost forever if we happen to eat a pork chop by mistake. The ancient Israelites could still receive forgiveness on that day, and their forgiven sins could be cleansed during the following year's Day of Atonement. But, although we can certainly receive forgiveness, there isn't another Day of Atonement on the horizon where our sins will be cleansed. This is it. As Hebrews 9:26 says, "But now, once at the end of the ages, He has appeared to put away sin by the sacrifice of Himself." Christ has entered into the Most Holy Place for the last time in His current capacity. His goal is to cleanse a people from their sins once and for all. Thus, it is plain to see that God cannot return to earth to claim His bride until He has finished cleansing the sanctuary—and His bride—from all her sins.

I realize that these ideas aren't very fashionable. Sin is pretty popular these days and has a fairly big cult following. In truth, many of us aren't all that bothered by its allurement; we're pretty happy with our present situation.

Others are just staunchly opposed to any idea that would propose some type of victory over sin for Christ's people. Sure, they may allow for occasional victory, but to suppose that a person can have total victory over sin all the time is just heretical. One of my professors was suggesting such an idea one day and I heard a young lady behind me mumble, "Oh, my goodness, I think he believes in perfection!" I was tempted to turn around and say to her, "Yeah, and so did Jesus." (See Matthew 5:48.) I refrained.

Sadly, many people are happy and content with an endless cycle of falling and being forgiven. We feel as though this is the zenith of the Christian experience: sinning, repenting, receiving forgiveness; sinning, repenting, receiving forgiveness. On and on it goes.

But certainly Christ has much more for His people. If His grace can't transform hearts and lives, what good is it? We're left with a bunch of forgiven people who are always falling down because they can't seem to get out of their own way. Jude 24 has good news for us, however. In unequivocal terms, Jude wrote a prayer to "Him that is able to keep you from falling" (KJV).

Jude doesn't write to the One who is able to endlessly keep forgiving us. To be sure, Christ can and will forgive us as long as we sincerely want Him to, but He has so much more for us than this. Instead of an endless cycle of falling down and being picked up, Christ wants to keep us from even falling in the first place. He wants to restore us to total newness of life. Surprisingly, many people think this is a bad thing, as if it were the worst news they have ever heard.

I don't know about you, but I enjoy total recovery. I'm not satisfied with partial mending. A few months ago, I suffered a thumb injury while playing flag football. At first I thought it was just a little sprain, but then I finally got it x-rayed and discovered that I had broken it pretty severely. Unfortunately, although the thumb healed significantly, it never made a full recovery. I don't have as great a range of motion, and if I bend it in certain directions, there is still significant pain, even after all this time.

Nagging injuries aren't fun. We certainly desire total recovery for our physical bodies, but many of us are satisfied with only partial recovery in the spiritual realm. Perhaps we even excuse our deficiencies by saying we are merely human.

But what I don't understand is this: Why is an idea that promises to improve the quality of a person's life viewed so negatively? Are we really in love with sin *that* much? If I were to come up to you and tell you that I had found a cure for the common cold, would you think that were a good thing? Granted, we are very skeptical these days about such gimmicks, especially as they relate to health, but Jesus' promise of total victory over sin is no gimmick. It's the Gospel in its fullest. He can free us from our sins, both their penalty and their power.

It reminds me of a story I once heard about a pastor that preached a sermon on sin one particular Sabbath. He kept stressing its terrible power over human beings and repeatedly said that humans couldn't enjoy total victory over it. Finally, in great frustration, an old woman stood up in the middle of his sermon and shouted, "Brother, stop glorifying sin!"

Indeed, we give sin far too much credit, as though it were the most powerful force in the universe. True, we are all sinners that have a natural craving for the dreadful disease, but Christ's grace is far more powerful than sin. As Romans 5:20 says, "But where sin abounded, grace did much more abound" (KJV). Although we are constantly surrounded by the gravity of sin, Christ's powerful grace is much stronger than any other force the universe has ever seen.

This explains why the 144,000 in Revelation 14 are described in such amazing terms. They are described as "the ones who follow the Lamb wherever He goes" and "in their mouth was found no deceit, for they are without fault before the throne of God" (Revelation 14:4, 5). This is not simply a description of a group of people who are covered with Christ's cloak of righteousness, all the while being totally dirty underneath. As we mentioned before, Christ's robe of righteousness is woven into their characters so that it becomes a part of who they are.

It should be plainly stated, however, that this perfect bride is never aware of her own perfection or sinlessness. The closer people get to Christ, the more unworthy and sinful they appear to themselves. This is what Isaiah said when he encountered God. With humility, he declared, "Woe is me, for I am undone! Because I am a man of unclean lips, and I dwell in the midst of a people of unclean lips; for my eyes have seen the King, the Lord of hosts" (Isaiah 6:5).

Neither is the bride obsessed with this idea of sinless perfection so that it's all she can focus on. Our job is not to wake up every morning and say, "I'm going to be sinless in everything I do." This simply results in an infatuation with self, which is antithetical to what perfection is all about. Our role is to simply follow the Lamb wherever He goes. Left to ourselves, we would fall flat on our faces, but when we follow Christ, He can take us to heights we never dreamed of reaching.

Roy Gane explained it best when he said,

> When I think about *becoming perfect in character*, I start contemplating my faults and become afraid. . . . But when I think of being *loyal to Christ*, the picture changes because my gaze is on Him. He is my example, shepherd, and guardian. I gain courage because all I need to do is follow Him where He wants to take me, including perfection of character.[2]

Many try to muddy the waters, however, by mistaking this with the idea of perfectionism. Whether intentional or not, they accuse those who believe in character perfection of teaching a "salvation by works" model. That is, perfectionism maintains that my salvation is dependent on my being perfectly sinless. Otherwise, I can't go to heaven.

Though I would not deny that many brands of this perfection theology seem to take this route, this is not what I'm saying at all. I don't believe that my views on this even remotely border on this type of legalistic mindset. No one's salvation is ever dependent on what he or she does. Perfection is not a person's ticket into heaven, no matter what time of earth's history that person lives in.

What I am saying, however, is that Christ's bride will have such an experience with Him that it will naturally lead to perfection of character. Those who live to see the Lord come would rather die than sin against their beloved Bridegroom.

I know that some may think these ideas reek of legalism—that total victory over sin is nothing more than a system of gaining salvation by works. But such a perspective is fundamentally flawed. If a person is motivated by the cross and a sincere desire to honor Christ, nothing her or she does is legalistic—including the complete discontinuation of placing dirty dishes in the heavenly sink. Legalism comes when a person does something—anything—to gain God's favor or His salvation. Desiring to work hand-in-hand with Christ in the total eradication of sin doesn't necessitate we revert to a legalistic paradigm.

In the end, Christ's bride will find total victory over sin, by faith. This will all come into focus when she realizes that every decision she makes is a reflection of her love for self, or her love for Christ. Ultimately, Christ's bride will allow the cross to take root in her heart and compel her to live fully for her Lover. But until that day, Christ can't return to claim a group that cares more about themselves than Him. He just can't. And He won't.

NOTES

1. Roy Gane, *Altar Call* (Berrien Springs, Mich.: Diadem, 1999), 330.
2. Ibid., 332.

CHAPTER XVII

RIGHTEOUSNESS 101

Perhaps you're overwhelmed by the previous chapter. It's a scary thought to realize that Christ has chosen to be dependent, in some ways, on His people on earth. We as human beings are naturally sinful, and to think that Christ's wedding depends on our getting over that; well, that's frightening.

There is also the danger of over-theorizing an issue. I have the tendency to do that, I know. I'm reminded of a cartoon I saw in *Reader's Digest* once that showed a couple of men working on some type of invention. The invention seemed to be working properly, but the caption underneath read, "Well, it works in practice; but what about in theory?" Those of us who enjoy sharpening our teeth on theology have the tendency to live in the theoretical, thinking that if we just know the right information, it will naturally lead to changed lives.

But I've realized something lately. I can have all the right theology and be convinced fully in my mind that Christ is looking for perfect people to represent Him on earth, but unless that makes a real change in my heart, it doesn't amount to a hill of beans. If the actions in my life don't reflect the theology in my head, I may as well believe in the Tooth Fairy. Christ is looking for loving Christians, not people who have all the right answers (though the two need not necessarily be separated).

With this being said, it doesn't mean we can abandon theological truths altogether. The right answers are still the right answers; and these are what should dictate my actions. I certainly can't expect my actions to rise above my theology. If I am convinced in my mind that there is no such thing as a Tooth Fairy, I'm not going to leave my tooth under the pillow at night. Neither will I come anywhere near character perfection if I don't believe it's possible—by God's grace—or see its relevance.

The truth is that perfection isn't just a pie-in-the sky idea. Even if everyone in the world agreed intellectually that we should strive for it, it wouldn't amount to much if unaccompanied by fruitage. So we must humbly fall before the Savior and ask for His true cleansing.

As I said earlier, you may be overwhelmed by the idea of living totally without sin. Many of us look at our lives and realize just how unworthy and sinful we are. It's easy to get discouraged and dejected. Some may have years of baggage that they have carried; others may be plagued by hereditary sins that have been passed down from generation to generation.

But the irony is, this is precisely where Christ wants us. He can't do much of anything with people who are feeling good about themselves and self-sufficient. That is precisely the root of sin. It is dependence on self. In order for Christ to truly use us as His vessels, we must come to the place where we feel totally broken and unworthy.

Thus, Carsten Johnsen wrote,

> The sanctified man is the man who is becoming perfectly whole because he is perfectly broken. I am speaking about the brokenness of heart, the contriteness of spirit. This is, from the day of justification on, supposed to be the one constant and all-absorbing attitude of man's every being.[1]

This is what the cross can do for us. Not only does it save us from the penalty and power of sin, but it also humbles us. It is supposed to lay man's glory in the dust. To think that Christ, the sinless Son of God, would willingly give up His life for sinners such as us is a very humbling thought. This certainly weighed heavily on the heart of Isaac Watts when he penned the words to his most well-known hymn,

> *When I survey the wondrous cross,*
> *On which the Prince of Glory died,*
> *My richest gain, I count but loss,*
> *And pour contempt on all my pride*

There is no way that a person can honestly look at the cross and have a sense of pride. The cross reveals the full weight of what our sinful choices do to God's Son. It's no wonder that Paul wrote to Timothy, "This is a faithful saying and worthy of all acceptance, that Christ Jesus came into the world to save sinners, of whom I am chief" (1 Timothy 1:15). Paul wasn't merely paying lip service to the idea that he was the "chief" of sinners; in light of the cross, he honestly felt that way.

It isn't until we reach this point that we can be used by God. In truth, until we are humbled by the cross, we won't even have the desire to be used by Him in the first place.

This is why Jesus said what He did in Mark. There we read His well-known words, "Whoever desires to come after Me, let him deny himself, take up his cross, and follow Me" (Mark 8:34). This is really the zenith of the Christian experience. Responding to Christ involves dying to self every day, taking up our cross, and following Him.

I wish I could tell you what this entails, but I can't. No two crosses are the same, and denying self is implemented differently by everyone. As much as we like to make blanket pontifications as to what other people should be doing, they may not be struggling with the same things we are. This is not to say that we throw out standards, but God hasn't appointed any of us to be the "Perfection Police." Well would it be for us to remember Christ's words in Matthew 7:5, "Hypocrite! First remove the plank from your own eye, and then you will see clearly to remove the speck from your brother's eye."

I fear, however, that many of us feel as though we have, in fact, taken the plank out of our own eye and are now fully justified and equipped to do eye surgery on our fellow believers. I am certainly not innocent of these crimes. I have attempted my fair share of eye surgeries in my day, feeling as though I have overcome my own blindness.

I don't believe this was the point of Christ's words though. While there is definitely a place to lovingly correct our brothers and sisters, it's not our job to play the role of the Holy Spirit and convict the world of sin.

Ultimately, where God wants us in this whole process is down on our knees, humbly bowing before His throne.

Taking up our cross involves submitting to the Creator and surrendering our will to Him. It's about handing the reigns over to Christ and asking Him to lead us wherever He desires.

Sometimes this takes shape in a practical way by simply asking the Lord, through prayer, to take our hearts and minds. There are times throughout my day when I just have to say to God, "Lord, I am a wretched sinner who is not worthy to be Your child. Take me. I surrender to You." This is nothing earth-shattering or even magical. But there is something about it that enables us, through God's grace, to take a step back and re-evaluate our actions. This then allows God to take hold of our lives and use us for His glory.

Of course, some may wonder what perfection looks like from a "practical" point of view. Unfortunately, there are many people who think that perfection is a check list; that when they have finally reached the bottom of their list—after they've stopped eating all dairy and thrown out their last rock n' roll CD—*then* they will be perfect.

Or, this check-list mentality may surface in more subtle ways—ways that are less characteristic of what so-called "conservative" people avoid. We may have the mindset that if we finally overcome our bad temper problem, *then* we will finally be perfect. Or we may think that if we finally start feeding the hungry or promoting world peace, *then* we will reach perfection.

While avoiding or doing all of these things may be good and noble—and probably have their place in the Christian's life—checking items off a list doesn't make a person perfect. Just when we think we've done it all, there will ever be something more that we've overlooked.

This is precisely what happened with the man we've come to know as the "Rich, Young Ruler." When he approached Jesus and asked him what he must do to gain eternal life, Jesus responded by telling him to keep the commandments. Feeling pretty smug about his behavior, the young man informed Jesus that he'd checked all these things off his list.

But there's more.

Jesus said to the young man, "If you want to be perfect, go, sell what you have and give to the poor, and you will have treasure in heaven" (Matthew 19:21). Christ's definition of perfection isn't a check list. Even though He tells the man to go and *do* something, He shows that this action was ultimately a reflection of the heart. He knew that the young man's heart was only about himself, and Christ wanted to show him that perfection comes in serving others.

And hence we see what perfection looks like in shoes. It's not having all the right theological answers; it's not abstaining from eggs; it's not even keeping the Sabbath. All these things, as praiseworthy as they may be, find their zenith in loving and serving others. It is little wonder then that Paul unequivocally wrote that "love is the fulfillment of the law" (Romans 13:10).

After all, this is the same picture that Christ painted in Matthew 5:48 when He encouraged His listeners to "be perfect, just as your Father in heaven is perfect." The context in which He said this is *agape* love. "You have heard that it was said, 'You shall love your neighbor and hate your enemy,' " Jesus said, "But I say to you, love your enemies, bless those who curse you, do good to those who hate you, and pray for those who spitefully use you and persecute you" (Matthew 5:43, 44).

Being perfect is the result of allowing Christ to make you perfect in this *agape* love.

Of course, being perfect in *agape* love isn't a replacement for keeping the Sabbath, or becoming a vegan, or any other doctrine we may maintain. Rather, when we allow Christ to perfect us in love, we understand that these things are only vehicles by which we can spread that *agape* love to others. The purpose of the health message is not simply to make us healthier or live longer per se, but to allow our bodies to be healthier so that we can be more loving to others.

This is the reason why I love Paul's words in Colossians 3:14 where he wrote, "But above all these things, put on love, which is the bond of perfection." We can talk about different standards all day long; we can take out our check list and see if we've reached "perfection" by human standards. But *agape* love is the glue that holds perfection together. Without it, all the other stuff just falls apart and travels aimlessly through the vast sea of ambiguity.

Thus, all of our so-called "standards" can only find their true meaning within the context of *agape* love. We can stand up at church and pontificate about how a person should not watch television if he or she wants to be perfect, but these ideas, divorced from *agape* love, are arbitrary at best and only cause spiritual bondage in the end. This is often manifested in some well-intentioned speaker standing up on Sabbath morning and preaching a 45-minute sermon, saying over and over again, "Television is bad, and you shouldn't watch it," and then sitting down. While not entirely untrue, such a presentation lacks the motivation of the Gospel.

But place these standards in the light of Calvary and in the context of *agape* love, and a person won't want to waste his or her time in front of a box that ultimately blunts the senses and robs a person of *agape* love. Not only does spending a couple of hours a day in front of a TV (or even a couple of hours a week) cause a person to become self-indulgent and unloving, but it is time that is taken away from being of useful and loving service to other people. This is entirely antithetical to *agape* love and, by way of conclusion, antithetical to what it means to be perfect.

As Sabbath-keeping, veggie-meat-eating, tithe-paying Christians, we, as Adventists, should be the most loving group of people there is. Of all churches, we should be known for our love. These standards that we so eagerly cling to should aid us towards being the most loving people on the planet. That is what perfection is all about.

Quite a few years ago now, my dad had a burden to start a church on Boston's south shore. The birthplace of President John Quincy Adams, the city of Quincy is a tough neighborhood that had virtually no Adventist presence.

So my dad, along with a Bible worker and a few other faithful pilgrims, set out to look for a church to rent where they could meet each Sabbath morning. They opened up the telephone book and contacted every single church that met in the city, only to be turned down again and again. After three or four months of searching, their efforts came up empty. As you can imagine, a lot of soul-searching went on during those few months, asking God whether it was His will to start a church in the city after all.

Finally, my dad got a hold of a Lutheran pastor who said he was willing to sit down and talk about the possibility of renting their church on Sabbath mornings. So my dad, along with his Bible worker, met with the pastor and a few of his board members—an older, retired couple—in the basement of the church. My dad explained to the pastor what they needed: four hours on Saturday mornings for church and then a couple hours one night a week for prayer meeting. The whole time, my dad and his Bible worker were praying in their minds, pretty much convinced that their requests would be fruitless.

To their surprise, after a few questions from the pastor and the retired couple, the pastor asked, "How much can you pay?" Baffled, my dad returned, "You mean you're going to rent to us?" The pastor replied, "Yes, but how much can you pay?"

With just a small group meeting at the time, there was not a lot of money for renting a church. Nevertheless, my dad humbly responded that they could pay only $50 a month— meager funds even in those days. Graciously, the pastor said that that would be fine, and as the congregation grew they could give as much money as they could afford. When they moved from the building and bought their own church eight years later, they were still paying only $300 a month.

A few weeks later, my dad came across the retired lady at the church. They ran a day care in the basement of the church, and she was there helping out with it. As my dad got to chatting with her, it soon became clear why this church—after all the other churches they had contacted were unwilling—had agreed to rent the church to them.

Apparently the lady had been a nurse at Quincy Hospital some years earlier. And when she had started working there—35 or 40 years earlier—there was a young man who was a doctor, doing his residency at the hospital. "You know, he made a profound impression on me," she said. "He was a wonderful Christian man. He was so kind-hearted and nice. And I remember a few things about him. I remember that he was single and all the nurses that were single were impressed with him. But I also remember that he was a Seventh-day Adventist and he didn't drink coffee." She continued, "But he left such an impression on me. He was such a tender-hearted and nice man."

He must have left quite the impression on her. Forty years later she still remembered him. And because of this encounter, a whole congregation was born. Because of the care and compassion of one man 40 years earlier, a whole church was raised up that subsequently led scores of other souls to Christ. All because of the seemingly innocent actions of one man who had responded to his Savior.

But as my dad stood there talking with the lady, the wheels started turning in his head, and something suddenly dawned on him. He couldn't help but ask, "Do you, by chance, remember that doctor's name?" The woman responded, "Oh, yes." Almost anxiously, my dad wondered, "What was his name?" She paused for a second and then replied, "His name was Dr. Ed Latimer."

What seemed like an innocent recollection to this lady was enormous to my dad. Her answer confirmed his hunch, and almost getting choked up he said to her, "That man later became my father-in-law."

The loving actions of my grandfather 40 years earlier paved the way to make it possible for my dad—who, at the time, may not have even been born yet in a small town in Eastern Canada, 500 miles away—to start a church that would continue such a legacy of love. I'm not trying to imply that my grandfather—as wonderful a man as he was—was the epitome of perfection, but I do believe, in some small way, he caught the vision of what it means to be perfect in love on a day-to-day level.

We too can catch such a vision. We can respond wholeheartedly to Calvary and, by faith, allow Christ to perfect us in His love. We may not accomplish magnificent works of holiness that will be heralded the world over, but we can, moment-by-moment, make other peoples' existence a little better because we have brought them the love of Christ.

It's no wonder that Christ, in unequivocal words, said, "By this all will know that you are My disciples, if you have love for one another" (John 13:35). This is the essence of perfection. This is the essence of Calvary. And this is what Christ is looking for from His people in these last days.

After all, *agape* love is the glue of perfection.

NOTES

1. Carsten Johnsen, *The Maligned God* (Sisteron, France: Untold Story Publishers, 1980), 187.

CHAPTER XVIII

DOES GOD NEED HELP?

Back in the mid-90s, a pastor friend of our family was holding some evangelistic meetings in Siberia. You've probably heard of this much-fabled place, no doubt, but you may not have any clue as to where it is. It is a region in western Russia that is often portrayed as a frozen tundra that looks as if it is on the other side of the moon. I'm not sure if Siberia really does fit this stereotype, since I've never been there myself, but rest assured that it is a long way from where we are, both geographically and culturally.

The meetings were going pretty well for this pastor, but as they progressed, he sensed that a few of the people were a little antsy. There seemed to be something weighing on their minds that needed to be addressed. Finally, after this went on for a few nights, one person took him aside and, through a translator, indicated that he wanted to talk with him. He, of course, obliged, fully expecting a deep theological question to be asked of him. The question was surprising, however.

In no uncertain terms, this man, living in Siberia, asked the one question that seemed to be weighing most heavily on the minds of everyone living in the area. He wondered, "Is O. J. guilty?"

The question was alarming, of course. Here he was, thousands of miles away from where O. J.'s court case was going on, in a place that seemed as if it were in the middle of nowhere, and they were caught up in all the hysteria of Simpson's trial. It just goes to show how far-reaching the trial was.

At the time, it was labeled the "Trial of the Century," and there hasn't really been one that has rivaled it since. Those of us from the United States certainly felt justified in calling it such, but this story goes to show just how far-reaching it really was.

The verdict in his trial is one of those "Where were you?" moments. Perhaps you can remember where you were when the verdict came in. Those words will be forever etched in our minds, "We the jury, in the above-entitled action, find the defendant, Orenthal James Simpson, *not guilty* of the crime of murder." It was 1995, and I was sitting in my high school history class as a freshman. We were, of course, tuned in to one of the zillions of channels that were carrying the trial. We weren't the only ones watching around the world though.

To be sure, Simpson's trial definitely caught the attention of the world. People from Los Angeles to Laos, from Boston to Beijing, turned their attention to this one global event. No other trial that has occurred on earth has received as much attention.

Except for one.

I've always wanted to be a painter; not the type that puts paint on houses, but one that puts it on canvas. Although I have jumped head first into the art of photography, it has been my dream to be a painter. For years I have said this. Occasionally I will tell a friend of mine—who is a brilliant painter—that I want him to teach me to be the same. We have even gotten so far as tentatively scheduling a time when he will teach me. But it never happens.

I can see the first painting I would do if I learned the art. But since I can't do that, I'll have to paint it with words for you. So, look with me for a second.

In my mind, I see a huge courtroom that's bigger than any courtroom I've ever been in. It certainly isn't empty. Hundreds of curious onlookers stare with vivid interest at what is unfolding. It doesn't take us long to realize that this trial is far greater than any trial that has previously taken place, even O. J.'s. As you look closer at the painting, you notice that the prosecuting attorney is extremely mad. He is red in the face and is scowling as he points angrily at the defendant. You can almost imagine him yelling at the top of his lungs with hatred as he presents the evidence against the defendant. He definitely wants this man to fry.

And then, as you inspect the painting even closer, you suddenly realize that the person in the witness stand bears a striking resemblance to someone you know. Baffled for a minute by the person's identity, it finally occurs to us who it is. With perplexity, you realize the person who has taken the witness stand is our self.

The reason you're in the witness stand causes more confusion, however. What are you doing there? Who are you testifying for or against? With piqued interest, you finally turn your attention toward the person sitting in the defendant's chair. And as you focus in closer, you see a bearded man wearing an orange jumpsuit. He is handcuffed and sitting quietly in front of the audience. All eyes are planted firmly on him. Indeed, the whole courtroom is curiously focused on this one man as he stands trial, especially as the prosecuting attorney hurls accusation after accusation against him. Each word that the attorney flings at him is met with a collective gasp from the audience.

And then it suddenly dawns on us who the defendant is. It is God.

Too far-fetched, you say? It's happened before. And much like the current trial that God is experiencing, He chose not to speak in His own defense then either. He waited for others to testify on His behalf.

Sadly, no one did. As Jesus went to trial, some of His closest companions cursed His name; others ran away—some even naked. He was painfully alone.

Have you ever thought about the idea of *God* actually being the One on trial? We as Adventists believe staunchly in the so-called, "Pre-Advent Judgment," but very few of us apply this judgment to God. In our minds, God is the One judging us, not the other way around.

Surprisingly, however, this idea of God being judged is not so farfetched in many people's minds. It was common, in fact, for Jews during the Holocaust to stage such an event. Nobel Peace Prize winner Elie Wiesel, who survived the brutality of Auschwitz and is now one of the most well-known Jewish authors, wrote a book entitled *The Trial of God*, which is based on such experiences at Auschwitz. Some of the older Jewish gentlemen actually staged "mock trials" where God was the defendant. He was accused of abandoning His people and breaking the covenant that He had made with them thousands of years before.

And such is the mindset of many other people. The jury is still out on God in their minds.

These ideas didn't originate in any human being's mind, however. Long before the world ever existed, Satan stood before the heavenly magistrate and flung accusations at God. Revelation 12:7 indicates that "war broke out in heaven: Michael and his angels fought with the dragon." The word for "war" is the Greek word *"polemos,"* from which we get the word "politics." This is what was going on in heaven. It was politicking at its finest, and it originated in the mind of Satan. It was never meant to be a part of the human experience.

Ultimately, God was forced to cast Satan out of heaven, and He flung him to earth. Ever since then, Satan has been the one "who deceives the whole world" (v. 9). He's been defaming God's character and making false accusations against Him.

This tells me that there is something far greater going on in the universe than my immediate context. One of the biggest problems within the Christian world is that we don't understand the cosmic implications of our existence. More than simply affecting my own personal salvation when I choose to follow God, I am actually influencing the conflict that is going on between Christ and Satan.

Ultimately, the focus of preparing for the wedding must turn our attention towards a greater good outside of ourselves. Thus, we don't put on Christ's wedding dress of righteousness simply so we can look good; we do it so Christ can look good.

One of the greatest tragedies in all of scripture is recorded in the book of Judges. Although I could refer to just about any part of Judges to make this point, there is a tiny passage near the beginning of the book that is second to none. In Judges 5:23 we read, "'Curse Meroz,'" said the angel of the Lord. "'Curse its inhabitants bitterly.'" These are strong words. It's not every day that we read such unequivocal terminology coming from the lips of God.

But what had this place known as "Meroz" done that was so bad? Why had it forced God to curse it? The verse explains, "Because they did not come to help the Lord, to help the Lord against the mighty" (NASB).

The idea sounds strange to our ears and leaves us a little uncomfortable. Does God actually need *help*? He is, after all, the almighty, all powerful, all knowing God. How could He possibly need help from something outside of Himself? What does He need help with?

I have been grappling with this very question for quite some time. Although I have whole-heartedly believed that there is some type of cosmic event that is taking place outside of this planet, it has been a struggle for me to wrap my mind around it.

Until recently. With the help of my friend Kyle, the issues have suddenly come into focus and are making more sense. Think about this.

Imagine that you are a being that lives on another planet far, far away from here. Life is good for you. Your surroundings are beautiful; you have wonderful friends and family; no disease or wickedness exists; you don't even have a need to eat veggie-meat. What's more, there are neighboring planets that also share the same joy. Everyone gets along beautifully with one another.

Best of all, however, you have a wonderful Creator that you are excited about. The interaction that He shares with you personally is marvelous. Everything He does is exceptionally perfect and beautiful.

But then one day you notice that your Creator-Friend is at it again. Just as before, He has taken on the role of Creator. This time, however, He makes a place called "Planet Earth." At first you're excited because you will have new friends to visit. After all, it's always exciting when someone new moves into the neighborhood. But soon after He's done creating the world, something alarming happens.

The beings on this planet aren't like the rest of the beings in the universe. There's something different about them. In fact, they seem to take part in activities that are completely opposite of what you know to be good and praiseworthy. Instead of following the loving ways of the Creator, they wreak havoc and defy Him. Instead of uplifting one another, they tear each other down and even go so far as to destroy life. All of a sudden, what was once a perfect universe has been tainted by the beings on this planet known as Earth. This one planet has single-handedly changed the equilibrium of the whole universe.

What a troubling predicament God has created!

I don't know about you, but there would be one question on my mind at this point, and it would be directed toward God. Sure, I know that God is basically good and loving, and He has His reasons for doing things, but there would still be a lingering question weighing heavily on my mind. I would be eager to ask God, "What on earth were you thinking when You created Earth?"

And this is the predicament that God finds Himself in. He needs to justify His reasons for creating this mess we know as Earth.

Of course, there are a few solutions to God's problem. He could very easily wipe the whole planet out and say, "Oops, I made a little mistake. Let me start all over again." But this would cause more questions in the minds of those in the universe—both the angels and the rest of its created beings. After all, if God simply did this to anyone who stepped out of line, what's to say He wouldn't do it again if someone else did the same? This would only promote obedience out of fear.

Satan would certainly jump at this opportunity as well. He would have a field day, accusing God of being unmerciful and unloving.

On the other hand, God can't simply ignore the problem altogether either. To allow human beings to continue to exist in this state would seriously jeopardize the whole universe. Beings on other planets would have serious questions as to why God ever created this world in the first place, as they probably do to some extent right now, anyway.

To put this whole concept in simpler terms, what would you think if your next-door-neighbor brought home a bunch of dogs that were notorious for biting people? Not only would you be afraid of the dogs, but you would also wonder about your neighbor. He would certainly have to justify himself for pulling such a stunt, especially if he was going to give the dogs free reign throughout the neighborhood.

Granted, to some extent God has "caged" us up for now. We don't have free reign to run around the neighborhood at this point. He's kind of partitioned this planet off with a wall so that the cancer doesn't spread to the rest of His creation. But eventually, when Christ returns the second time, He is going to let us out. How does the rest of the universe know we're not going to bite them?

I'm sure some could object that this will all be laid to rest when our sinful natures turn into sinless natures at Christ's return. But this wouldn't be satisfying to the universe. After all, it was in this sinless state that Adam, the first human being, sinned. The universe needs assurance that human beings won't mess up again. They need assurance that God knew what He was doing when He created this planet and that He knows what He's doing by setting us free. Thus, His reputation is on the line.

Of course, I'm sure God has explained the plan of salvation to the rest of the universe, and they've certainly seen God's amazing love at Calvary. But the last part of the plan—you know, the part where God's grace transforms the lives of human beings, and we live up to the high standards that other created beings live up to—has yet to come to fruition. No wonder Paul wrote, "The creation waits in eager expectation for the sons of God to be revealed" (Romans 8:19, NIV).

With this thought in mind Carsten Johnsen wrote, "Obedience is the highest praise man can offer to God. In being obedient he vindicates God. And in vindicating the Other One, he vindicates himself."[1] More than any song we can sing or any dance we can break into, the highest praise a man can offer God is an obedient heart. The words we sing are empty—indeed, they are blasphemous—if our lives don't match their declarations. We must look pretty silly to other created beings when we limit our "praise" to singing. They must say, "Wow, those people can sing really loud and they can sway back and forth impressively, but their lives don't really match their words."

This is the reason Paul wrote in 1 Corinthians 4:9, "For it seems to me that God has put us apostles on display at the end of the procession, like men condemned to die in the arena. We have been made a spectacle to the whole universe, to angels as well as to men" (NIV). The word for "spectacle" is literally "theater." The whole universe has gathered around this planet just like people go to a theater to watch a play. They are eager to see how it will unfold. No wonder Shakespeare wrote, "All the world's a stage and we are mere players."

It's an amazing thought. God has placed His reputation in our hands. The part we play on this grand theater stage is a true reflection of our Director God. This should be enough to turn our thoughts from our own situation and judgment and onto God's. Righteousness by faith, then, takes on a greater context when we realize this. We are motivated to live righteously by faith so that Christ can be vindicated through our actions. The universe will then see that, indeed, God's reason for creating this planet is justified.

The beauty of this idea is that when we turn our attention to a greater cause, our actions not only make God look good, but they, by way of logical conclusion, make us look good as well. The universe will understand that God is not only good and trustworthy, but that we, as people who will be coming to a neighborhood near them very soon, are also good and trustworthy. Of course, we are never motivated by this, of vindicating ourselves, but it's the natural result of living to vindicate God.

The rest of the universe isn't the only place where the jury is still out on God, however. As I somewhat alluded to earlier, people on this planet certainly have questions about Him as well. Ever since time began, people have been questioning God and whether He is truly loving. All the wars, natural disasters, and other such things have certainly solidified the doubts in these people's minds.

Just yesterday, in fact, I was handed a piece of paper by a woman named Joanne who has more questions about God than you can shake a stick at. I am helping out with a Revelation seminar, and when we visited this lady to invite her back to the meetings, she revealed to us that she had a whole list of questions she wanted us to answer.

When I saw her at the meeting the next week, she handed me a typed piece of paper with 10 very articulate and poignant questions, labeled, "Questions that nobody ever talks about." I'm sure these are just the tip of the iceberg in her mind. And as I suspected, her questions didn't revolve around the identification of the second beast in Revelation 13, or whether 144,000 is a literal number. They went much deeper. She wondered things such as, "Why does God allow all his people to be crushed and tormented?" and, "If man is created in God's image and man is innately evil, what does that say about God?" In short, they were questions about God's character.

Do you think that God will simply sit back passively and wait until the millennium is over so that this lady's eyes will be enlightened? I can't imagine Him saying, "Too bad for you. You should have studied your Bible more." Perhaps, when the words on a page don't make sense to this lady, she will read about God's character through us.

Similarly, much of the bloodshed that this world has experienced has come at the hands of those who claim to follow God. We have, much like Israel of old, "profaned" God's name "among the nations" (Ezekiel 36:21). We have brought such shame to God's name that most people shudder when they hear the word "Christian."

Will God have a word in these last days, or will He remain silent? I'd like to think that before His Second Coming, His loving character will be seen in the lives of His followers, thus vindicating His name to the nations. At that point, people will truly understand who God is and what He's all about. They will truly see His love as reflected in us and be able to make an informed decision about Him: whether they want to follow or reject Him.

I love the words in a song by the group, *Casting Crowns*. They certainly cause me to think. With amazing clarity, lead singer Mark Hall, wonders, "If we are the body, why aren't His arms reaching?" It's a poignant question. We can talk about God all we want, but until we, as the body, actually reach out to those who Christ died for, people will never see a true picture of what God is like.

I'm also reminded of a sobering inscription that was found on the wall of a bunkhouse in a German concentration camp after World War II. Through all of the bloodshed, pain, and sorrow, someone wrote:

> *I believe in the sun - even when it does not shine.*
> *I believe in love - even when it is not shown.*
> *I believe in God - even when He does not speak.*

Maybe, just maybe, when it seems that God is silent, He is, instead, speaking through us. We have a tremendous opportunity—indeed, privilege—to be the shining examples of who God is. And in thus doing, we vindicate His name before the world and the universe.

Do you want take part in that awesome privilege? God has placed His reputation on the line and put it squarely in our hands—both before the universe, and this planet we call home. Are we going to vindicate God's faith in us? Will the whole universe see us and say, "Oh, so *that's* what He made them for. *That's* why He died for them and has let them be a part of society again"?

It's an amazing thought; that the equilibrium of the whole universe is riding on the outcome of this planet. God is waiting eagerly for His character to be reproduced in our lives. When this happens and we vindicate His name before the universe and the world, then, and only then, can He come.

NOTES

1. Johnsen, 267.

CHAPTER XIX

THE OFFENSIVE GOSPEL

I have to warn you: You may not like me after this chapter. Truthfully, I may not like myself either. But it's time we were honest with ourselves. I've tried my hardest to be flowery so far, framing the ideas I've shared in the least offensive way I can. I haven't wanted to offend anyone.

What many of us fail to understand, however, is that the Gospel can be, in all honesty, extremely offensive. Too many times we are handed the Gospel message in a cute little package. I've heard—and preached, I'm sure—dozens and dozens of "warm, fuzzy" sermons.

I was talking with a friend of mine just recently, in fact, who was praising a member of his church who often preached. My friend enjoyed this gentleman's preaching so much because, in his words, "He makes me feel good about who I am." Although I understand where my friend is coming from, the Gospel isn't supposed to make us feel good about who we are. It's supposed to humiliate us and bring us crawling on our knees to the cross, grateful that God loves us despite our shortcomings.

It's very sobering to actually read Jesus' words that are recorded in the Gospels. For every thought that He shared that revealed His gracious and merciful character, there are just as many that cut to the heart that are supposed to help us realize our true condition. He, Himself, declared, "Do not think that I came to bring peace on earth. I did not come to bring peace but a sword" (Matthew 10:34). If we read the Bible or hear a sermon that doesn't pierce our hearts, we're not getting the right message.

This is why Jesus proclaimed what He did to the Laodicean church. While He affirmed the previous six churches in some way or another—before constructively criticizing them—He did no such thing for the church in Laodicea. He didn't say, "You're doing a good job in this area, but..." He simply said, "I know your works, that you are neither cold nor hot" (Revelation 3:15).

171

The truth is, He needed to cut to the chase with the Laodiceans and He needs to do the same with us. Time doesn't permit for an awards banquet. There is serious work to be done. The problem with the Laodiceans, anyway, was pride. They already had a healthy opinion of themselves; their self-esteem was at an all-time high. It's generally not a good idea to give people with huge egos another compliment. It's just feeds their ego and swells their head.

Thus, Jesus, who describes Himself as the "Amen, the Faithful and True Witness," declares to the Laodicean church, "I will vomit you out of My mouth. Because you say, 'I am rich, have become wealthy, and have need of nothing'—and do not know that you are wretched, miserable, poor, blind, and naked" (Revelation 3:16, 17).

It's time we stop beating around the bush and get serious with ourselves. We should be extremely grateful that the Lord has pointed out in us that which we are unable to see about ourselves. In His mercy and love He has done this for us. He wants to save us from the embarrassment of showing up to the wedding in such a state.

I realize that it is fairly popular these days to be critical of the Adventist church; some people even make a living off it. My wish is not to add another voice to the negativity that permeates throughout the church, but to encourage the church as a whole to evaluate itself in light of what the Lord has shared in scripture. I have a positive outlook about where God wants to lead this church. I believe He wants to take us to heights that we have never dreamed possible. This is not an arrogant or triumphal attitude I speak with; Adventists are no better than any other church or denomination. God doesn't love us any more. But He *has* given us the awesome responsibility of revealing His present truth to this world.

But to get to that point, we must do some serious soul-searching. We merely have a form of godliness at this point, but we don't have the real thing. I fear that we as a people are guilty of the same thing Israel of old was; we are bowing our knee to Baal. It's frightening to realize, for example, how many hours of TV the average churchgoer watches each week. In his book, *Serve God, Save the Planet*, Matthew Sleeth claims that by the time the average American turns 71, he or she will have spent "a solid ten waking years sitting in front of a television"[1] Did you catch that? *Ten years!* Ten years of unproductive and fruitless "activity" that could have been used to better society and God's kingdom.

I fear that Adventists are not all that far behind; some even lead the pack. Many of us can quote more movie lines than Bible verses. Truthfully, we may not go to bars or parties, but we certainly participate vicariously through those who do on TV.

Some of us, on the other hand, devote more attention to the Sports section of the newspaper than to the Word of God. We spend more time talking about LeBron, A-Rod, or Beckham than we do Paul, Moses, or Jesus. The stadium has become our church, and we are far more willing to shell out $80 for a box seat—or $150 for the NFL Sunday Ticket—than put a few dollars in the offering plate to help God's work.

Those of us who may be abstaining from these "ungodly" vices may have reason to feel pretty good about ourselves. But we're no better. Pride may be our biggest problem. While our fellow Christians indulge in these sinful activities, we stand tall in self-righteousness. We feel as if we're doing pretty well because we have been vegans for 10 years, and we don't go out to eat on Sabbath afternoons. But, while we may follow the Bible perfectly, we are the most unloving and miserable people the world has ever seen.

Meanwhile, the Devil has the church-at-large jumping through hoops all the time. He has us fighting over issues, such as music and women's ordination. Although we are sincere in our desires to promote truth in these areas, the Devil has us simply re-arranging the deck chairs on the *Titanic*. We are majoring in minors. We squabble with one another over these issues as the rest of the world perishes for lack of a Word from the Lord.

Most of these things have caused us to neglect the mission that God has given us: to proclaim the Three Angel's Messages and to prepare a people to meet the Lord. In reality, we only pay lip-service to one of the most fundamental aspects of our identity: Christ's Second Coming. When it boils down to it, we're not all that anxious for Christ's wedding to take place.

You may think it sounds ridiculous when I say this. Oh, we sing "Never Part Again" at the end of every camp meeting (at least my conference does) and we preach our sermons on heaven and the Second Coming every once in a while. Of course we want Christ to return! But don't you think, with all sincerity, that if we *truly* wanted Christ to return, we would cooperate with Him a little more than we currently do?

When it comes right down to it, if we were to be honest with ourselves, most of us would prefer Christ to come when we are about 75. We want to enjoy all this life has to offer first, with heaven as the cherry on top. We want to get married, have kids, enjoy a productive career, buy a nice house, receive a little recognition from our peers, go on a Caribbean cruise every once in a while, have fun with our grandkids, and play golf in Florida when we've retired. We may even want to be active members in our local church.

In truth, however, we care more about our temporal happiness than God's eternal happiness.

How many times have you heard someone ask, for example, "Is it wrong to say that I want to get married or have grandchildren before Jesus comes?" This is certainly a pretty innocent question that many of us have asked. But the very root of the question reveals a person's true motivation and concerns. We would rather enjoy our "happiness" at the cost of delaying Christ's.

Don't get me wrong, every once in a while, when facing difficult times or on our death bed, we say we want Christ to return. At that point, however, we want Him to return for selfish reasons. We want to escape our toil and misery and enjoy the pleasures of heaven. Not once do we stop and realize, though, that perhaps Christ is waiting at the altar for us, anxious for our grand appearance. He's left wondering when we're going to get our act together and show up.

Not too long ago I was sharing some of these frustrations with a friend of mine. As I mentioned earlier, although I may sound cynical or negative regarding the state that the church is in, I still believe that this church is God's Remnant that He has ordained to reveal His character to the world. I am, in no way, superior to anyone else when it comes to these problems. More than simply saying I am guilty by association, I definitely contribute in a proactive way to our unfortunate condition.

Just the same, I can also be a part of the solution, as can you. We're all in this together, every one of us. Just as surely as we have let the Lord down, we can, as a corporate group of believers, fulfill His high calling and prepare a people for the marriage of the Lamb.

When I shared these ideas with my friend, his response caught me off guard, however. He asked me, point blank, "So what's the solution?" More than simply debating about the theoretical, he wanted to know what my practical solution was for a church that has a Laodicean problem.

As I said earlier, I like to live in the theoretical, for the most part. Thus, I was at a loss for words when he asked me this question. I didn't have an answer for him. I was stumped. It became the theme of contemplation for the rest of my day.

Now, I know that there are many people in the church who have different ideas about what's going to "finish the work." Whether consciously or not, that which we emphasize and talk about the most reveals what we think the Big Solution is. Many of us think the solution is women's ordination, or vegetarianism, or holistic small groups, or whatever other pet idea we may espouse. Some of us act as though if women could just be ordained, or the whole church stopped eating cheese, then the Lord would return.

Others may call for legalistic reform. *If we could just get everyone to trash their TVs*, some may think, *then true revival can take place.* I'm not saying that there isn't a need for such an action. Perhaps God has convicted you on this subject, or a similar subject, in order for you to grow in Him. Truthfully, this book probably wouldn't have reached chapter three if I had a TV.

What I am saying, however, is that these types of things aren't the Big Solution. They may be tiny answers, but they are merely symptoms of a bigger problem.

I don't want to diminish them at all, but these issues are merely superficial and symptomatic of a deeper problem. They must always be discussed in the context of the Great Controversy and preparing people to meet the Lord. They are not ends in themselves. Too many times we get caught up in presenting them as the be-all and end-all of Christianity. They are not.

So women get ordained. Then what?

We all become vegans. And then?

As I pondered the question that my friend had posed to me, it all of a sudden dawned on me what the answer was. And it is far simpler than I could have imagined. In many senses, we all know the answer. We have read it a million times in the Bible, but have not given it enough thought or credence.

The Bible is saturated with this idea. Whenever God called His people back to Him, He told them to do this. It is also at the heart of the message to the Laodicean church. After revealing to the church its true condition, Jesus petitions in unmatched vigor, "Therefore, be zealous and repent" (Revelation 3:19).

The answer is repentance.

You can't escape this idea. All of scripture reveals as much. Whenever God called His people back to Himself in the Old Testament, repentance was the answer. John the Baptist, who was the forerunner of Christ at His first coming, proclaimed repentance as well. Acts tells us that when Peter preached on Pentecost, his listeners "were cut to the heart, and said to Peter and the rest of the apostles, 'Men and brethren, what shall we do?'" (Acts 2:37). Peter replied, "Repent!" (v. 38).

It would certainly seem fitting that as John the Baptist admonished repentance as the preparation for Christ's first coming, so this would also be the first step in preparing the bride for Christ's Second Coming. It would also seem fitting that, as we wait for the latter rain, we follow what the apostles did during the former rain. Then, and only then, can Christ do with us what He intends. We can't overcome our problems if we don't acknowledge that we have them.

Repentance isn't just a personal experience, however. Although it starts with us as individuals, Jesus' message of repentance to the Laodiceans was sent to the whole church, starting with the leaders and moving on down.

It reminds me of two individuals in the Old Testament. The first one was Daniel, who cried out to the Lord three times, "We have sinned!" (See Daniel 9.) Although he could have certainly rested in knowing that he was doing pretty well for himself, Daniel took the guilt of the whole Israelite nation upon himself and pleaded to the Lord on their behalf. He repented for the people as a whole.

The second individual that comes to mind is the king of Nineveh. When Jonah proclaimed God's judgment to that city, the king "arose from his throne and laid aside his robe, covered himself with sackcloth and sat in ashes," and he published a decree saying that every man and beast should be "covered with sackcloth, and cry mightily to God; yes, let every one turn from his evil way and from the violence in his hands" (Jonah 3:6, 8). The king responded with repentance and had his people do the same.

You may think that I have finally shown my hand or that you have uncovered my "hidden agenda" after 18 chapters. I'm really a raging lunatic who has an unpopular and self-righteous message to share. In all honesty, however, I had no intention of discussing this issue when I started writing this book. It has only been since I started writing this book that I've come to the serious realization that this has always been God's answer to His peoples' problem. Quite simply, we cannot grow until we first acknowledge our departure from God;

neither can we prepare for the wedding until we first realize and admit our nakedness.

It's kind of ironic, in a way. As a young child, probably no more than three or four years old, I used to walk around my house with a little Bible in my hand yelling, "Repent! Repent! Repent!" I'm not sure why I would do it, but I would say this to my brother and sister; to my dogs or cats; to anyone or anything that would listen. Little did I realize, however, the seriousness of this idea.

God is calling His people to repentance. In unequivocal terms, He says to the Laodicean church, "Therefore, be zealous and repent." Although it's somewhat offensive, it's also the Gospel. Will we humble ourselves and acknowledge our departure from God? Will we admit that we do, indeed, have a problem?

His wedding depends on it. His goodness leads us to it.

> *Lord: Thank You that, in Your mercy, You have pointed out our faults to us. May we respond to You with our whole hearts, humbling ourselves as a corporate body and acknowledging the fact that we have departed from You. As a people, help us to fulfill Your high calling. Make us dissatisfied with the status quo and lead us to repentance. This is our prayer, in Jesus' name, Amen.*

NOTES

1. J. Matthew Sleeth, *Serve God, Save the Planet* (Grand Rapids, Mich.: Zondervan, 2006), 109.

CHAPTER XX

Driving along Storrow Drive in Boston—the road that runs alongside the beautiful Charles River—there used to be a sign that was somewhat infamous. I still remember seeing it as a kid and being amused by it. For years it was an identifiable mark on this stretch of road. The sign was an advertisement for the Charles River Apartments and simply said, "If you lived here, you'd be home by now."

Quite a deep concept, I know. Yet there is a certain depth to the obvious statement it makes.

I wonder, however, if we could spin the phrase just a little bit to fit our current predicament. Based on what we have discussed in this book, I wonder if we could change the statement to say, "If we believed, we'd be home by now."

This is not meant to be a cute little cliché that we repeat every once in a while, nor is it a slogan or a marketing ploy. This is a real issue that we must grapple with. I realize it is a scary thought to acknowledge that we have a part to play in hastening Christ's Second Coming. This idea isn't all that popular. It requires us to change the way we are currently living; to reach above the status quo.

I was sharing this idea with one of my friends recently, and he, somewhat tongue-in-cheek, replied, "I don't agree with that idea, but that's probably because I don't want to give up my current lifestyle. I like watching my TV." Although he said it jokingly, I think he revealed the mindset of many of us, myself included. The issue isn't only TV, of course; it's just one of many things that may plague us (though, admittedly, it seems as though I have been harping on that subject quite a bit in this book). The fact is, we are extremely happy with the status quo and strive for a life of relative comfort.

One of the saddest pages in Israel's history came on the edge of the Promised Land. You know the story, I'm sure, but it's worth revisiting. God instructs Moses to send 12 men to spy out the land of Canaan. So Moses carefully selects one man from each tribe and sends them to check out the land, to see whether the land is good or bad, and whether the people who dwell in it are strong or weak, few or many.

You can imagine the anticipation the rest of Israel must have felt as the 12 men were gone. It was for this purpose that God brought them out of Egypt. They had visions of milk and honey. They could taste it in their mouths. Never before had they enjoyed such a life, and it was all going to be theirs.

Sure enough, when the spies returned to the people, their report matched the imagination of every Israelite. With veiled excitement, the spies announced, "We went to the land where you sent us. It truly flows with milk and honey" (Numbers 13:27). They even brought back some luscious grapes from the Promised Land, causing the mouths of every person to salivate with delight.

But that wasn't all they said about the Promised Land. With consternation and concern, 10 of the spies declared, "Nevertheless the people who dwell in the land are strong... We are not able to go up against the people, for they are stronger than we" (Numbers 13:28, 31). This report sent the Israelite camp into shock waves. While the spies painted the most glorious picture of what their future home was like, it all came crashing down when they revealed the great giants that they would have to go up against.

Before the negativity could carry on too long, however, Caleb piped up and proclaimed, "Let us go up at once, and take possession, for we are well able to overcome it."

By the time Caleb said this, though, it was already too late; the people were discouraged beyond belief. Whereas just a few days before, they were excited and eager to enter the Promised Land, they were now discouraged to no end. Nothing Caleb or Joshua could say would allay their fears. The report that the 10 other spies gave was enough to weaken their faith in God's ability to help them overcome. And the rest, as they say, is history.

Although the Children of Israel had a momentary reform—after God declared that none of them would enter the Promised Land except for Caleb and Joshua—it was all down hill from there. They wandered in the desert for the next 40 years. Caleb and Joshua were the only two original Israelites that entered into Canaan alive.

It's easy to see our own history in Israel's. The Lord wanted to bring us into the Promised Land a long time ago. But because of our unbelief, we have gotten in our own way and kept ourselves out of that heavenly land. And amid all this—at the heart of the Israelite's refusal to enter the Promised Land—one of the most sobering and profound questions is uttered from the lips of God, "How long will these people reject Me?" (Numbers 14:11). Rightfully so, our refusal to enter the Promised Land is not just a rejection of heaven, it's a rejection of the Person who dwells there.

As we sit on the border of the Promised Land, we have an awesome opportunity to take part in one of the greatest events ever accomplished in the whole universe. There have been many great witnesses for God in past ages. The "Hall of Faith," recorded in Hebrews 11, shares the stories of a few of those people who have been lights for God in their own spheres. People such as Enoch, Abraham, Moses, and David were tremendous champions of what God accomplished through those who devoted themselves to Him. This chapter doesn't even mention New Testament characters, such as John, Stephen, or Paul.

But the last two verses in the chapter reveal something very interesting. After alluding to the many witnesses who have gone before, the author of Hebrews wrote, "And all these, having obtained a good testimony through faith, did not receive the promise, God having provided something better for us, that they should not be made perfect apart from us" (Hebrews 11:39, 40).

How could there be something better for us? What could that be?

Quite simply, instead of having a few scattered individuals who have stood tall for God, there is going to be a whole generation of people that fully surrender to Him and reveal His character to the world and universe.

Psalm 14 speaks beautifully about this. If ever there was a chapter that addresses our present situation, it is this chapter. It so wonderfully illustrates the gulf between the righteous and the unrighteous.

David begins the chapter by saying, "The fool has said in his heart, 'There is no God'" (Psalm 14:1). He continues, "The Lord looks down from heaven upon the children of men, to see if there are any who understand, who seek God. They have all turned aside, they have together become corrupt; there is none who does good. No, not one" (vv. 2, 3). It's a sobering commentary on the condition of the world today.

Yet at the heart of the chapter, David wrote with confidence, "For God is with the generation of the righteous" (v. 5). Could it be that amid an era in which God is so unashamedly bashed and slandered, there would be a whole generation of people who lived righteously for Him? I believe that it is possible. And it can be fulfilled in us.

We have a tremendous opportunity to be a part of a generation that finally shows up to the marriage of the Lamb. It is something that has never happened before in this universe's history. This is why the author of Hebrews finished his Hall of Faith by writing that those who have gone before us will "not be made perfect apart from us." As righteous as those people were, they fell short of the prize. But now, through us, they can be perfected when Christ returns.

As an entire generation responds wholeheartedly to God by faith, Christ will accomplish in us what He has never been able to do before. He will have an entire generation of people who follow Him wherever He goes. He will have an entire generation of people that perfectly reflect His character of love, thereby avoiding those things that bring dishonor to His name. And through this, He will be vindicated before the world and the universe.

Perhaps it sounds scary, and it should. Christ is inviting us to go where no generation has gone before. Not only is He calling us to heaven, but He is calling us to fit ourselves fully *for* heaven. This is a frightening thought. But amid the overwhelming fear that may strike our hearts, there is also wonderful news. We can be a part of the most exciting movement the universe has ever witnessed.

Maybe you don't want to take part in it, and that's fine. God isn't going to keep you out of heaven for such an attitude. Your salvation is not dependent upon living perfectly. You can continue on with business as usual, live your 84.5 years that Adventist vegetarians live, die a peaceful death, and be raised again at the resurrection. Christ will eventually come with or without your help.

But maybe you're tired of the status quo. Maybe you're tired of going through the motions of your Christian experience. And maybe, just maybe, it would be exciting to—instead of taking the underground route to heaven— be part of a generation of people that glorifies God and finally vindicates His name before the entire universe. I can't think of any greater joy than making the most important Person in my life look good.

Truthfully, it would be refreshing to know that we can be part of a greater cause, to know that God has placed the destiny of the entire universe in our tiny little hands. Not ours alone, of course, but a whole generation of people that follow the Lamb into the marriage room.

It is important to realize, then, that this endeavor is a corporate pursuit. Although we may feel as though we are doing our part in God's cause, we have to understand that we're not alone. Christ's bride is a whole group of people, not just scattered individuals. When the Children of Israel stood on the border of the Promised Land, it wasn't as if God said, "All right, I'm going to let Caleb and Joshua come in, but the rest of you have to wander around the wilderness for another 40 years." Neither did He invite a few tribes into Canaan while exiling the rest. It was all or nothing.

The same applies to us. We're all in the same boat; we're all in this together. Christ will not return until He has a corporate group of believers that prepare themselves collectively for the wedding.

Some may object, I'm sure, that it sounds as if God has different standards of living for different generations. Why does God expect perfection of us, but not those who have lived in previous generations?

The truth is that God has always expected and desired perfection from His people. His standards of righteousness have always been the same. Only now, however, has He given us light to understand this. Certainly God couldn't reveal this to His followers of old when they were struggling with things such as polygamy or idolatry. Slowly over time, however, He has revealed more and more truth to His people, but only as much as they can handle at one time. As Acts 17:30 indicates, "Truly, these times of ignorance God overlooked, but now commands all men everywhere to repent."

You may not think that this is fair, but I don't think God has ever wanted people in heaven who are looking to do the minimum, anyway. Such an attitude reveals the true affections of the heart. If I simply tried to get by with the minimum in my relationship with my wife, I would seriously have to re-evaluate my affections toward her. Those who have sincerely responded to Christ by faith will ever be asking what more they can do for Him. A heart that is truly stirred by Christ's *agape* love knows no bounds.

It's not that God has any higher standard for us now, or that He loves us anymore, or that we're better than other generations; it's just that sooner or later there will be a people who finally respond to Christ with their whole hearts. They will withhold no part of themselves from Him. It will be full surrender. They will say, as did Caleb and Joshua, "Let us go up at once and take possession, for we are well able to overcome it" (Numbers 13:30).

Is there a Caleb? Is there a Joshua among us? Who will champion the cause?

I love the words that were spoken to Dwight L. Moody as he set sail from England to America after one of his overseas trips. With piercing sincerity, one man said to Moody, "The world has yet to see what God will do with... the man who is fully and wholly consecrated to Him." The words cut to Moody's heart, and he responded by saying, "By God's help, I aim to be that man."[1] I don't know if Moody succeeded or not, but imagine what God could do with a *whole generation* of men and women fully devoted and consecrated to Him. We could, as did the apostles, turn the world upside down.

Not to be outdone, the great English revivalist, John Wesley, once said, "Give me one hundred men who hate nothing, but sin and love God with all their hearts, and I will shake the world for Christ!"[2] What an awesome thought! Is it possible for such a thing to happen; that there could be a hundred men or women who hate nothing but sin and love God with all their hearts so that the world can be shaken for Christ? What about a whole generation?

God believes as much, and He waits longingly at the altar for such a movement to take place.

My wife and I witnessed an interesting series of events at a wedding that we recently attended. Until then, I had only heard or read about such things happening. I was delighted to experience it first-hand this time, however.

It was one of our friend's weddings that took place in the chapel of the Seminary. As people typically do when they go to a wedding, we arrived a few minutes early, signed the guest book, and found a seat next to a few people we knew. As we sat and talked for a few minutes, the preliminary music played in the background, delighting our souls.

Then the moment arrived. The families of the bride and groom were seated, grandparents first and then the parents. The wedding party marched down and took their places. And then, something I had never witnessed before, the groom marched down by himself and took his place.

And then it happened. With piqued interest, everyone turned toward the back of the church in eager anticipation of seeing the bride. But something funny happened. She wasn't there. I'm sure most of us thought she was simply adding a little drama to the event, as if a bride needs to be even more dramatic in her grand entry, but the few seconds of drama turned into a few minutes. You could feel a sense of nervousness envelope the crowd. People started wiggling in their seats. Two minutes turned into three, and three minutes into four. Still, there was no sign of the bride.

By this time I'm sure the groom was dying inside. He probably thought to himself, *Surely this can't be happening to me.* In truth, no groom ever wakes up in the morning and says to himself, "Well, this is the day that I get left at the altar." It's just not at the forefront of anybody's mind.

Of course, the audience started looking around, whispering things to one another. It seemed as though no one had any idea where the bride was. I think it would be safe to say that a good five minutes passed before there was any sign of her.

And then, all of a sudden, there she was, standing in all her glory and beauty at the back of the church. You could almost hear a collective sigh of relief when she appeared. The bridal processional started playing and everyone stood to their feet, all eyes fixed firmly upon the bride as she marched down the aisle.

It is usually at this point that I like to turn my attention elsewhere. Instead of looking at the bride, as most people do, I like to look at the groom. The expression on the groom's face is pretty revealing, as I'm sure it was on my face when I got married. Sometimes you can see the wheels turning inside his head. It's almost as if some guys think, *Oh, no. What have I gotten myself into?* Most guys, of course, are absolutely excited about what they see coming down the aisle.

And this is precisely the expression that was on this groom's face. There was joy; there was relief; there was excitement; but most of all, there was a smile. In fact, he was all smiles. The young lady who meant the most to him was finally marching down the aisle and into his life for eternity. What greater joy can a man experience than this?

I can't help thinking of Christ's glorious wedding. Forgive me for doing so. But He too has been waiting at the altar for His delayed bride. He is nervous with anticipation. He is excited beyond belief. And, although we are late to the wedding, He will still love us when we finally do show up. And when we finally do appear at the back of that church, He will be all smiles also.

I don't know about you, but that makes me excited: to imagine the smile on Jesus' face when His bride finally prepares herself and shows up at the wedding to join her life to His. Imagine the joy in Jesus' heart when Ephesians 5:27 is finally fulfilled and He can "present to Himself a glorious church, not having spot or wrinkle, or any such thing, but that she should be holy and without blemish." How excited Christ will be when He can proclaim far and near that He has the most beautiful bride the universe has ever seen!

That thought alone would motivate me enough to do all I can to be part of a group of people who finally show up for the wedding. It would motivate me to respond wholeheartedly to the Groom who shed His blood unconditionally for me. Will you do the same?

I hope this book isn't just another book that you've read. Maybe you've been a little amused by some of the stories I have shared, or you were even forced to look again at some of the beliefs you espouse. If that is all this book has done, however, I feel as if I have failed in many ways. It has been my prayer that something in this book has gripped your heart and caused you to reevaluate your own life. I hope it has caused you to reflect upon your own motivations and brought you to the foot of the cross, sincerely asking God to use you in a mighty way. Don't be satisfied with business as usual. Time has lingered on long enough.

Truthfully, the implications of God's present predicament are too serious for us to maintain the status quo. There's no time to write just "another book" that tickles our hearts, but doesn't bring us to our knees in conviction. The world is passing away while God waits at the altar.

So I ask you, friend: Will we, as a corporate body of believers, fully surrender to Christ? Will we finally come to the altar and join ourselves to Him? I hope so. And so does God.

But until then, He eagerly waits.

When we finally do show up, I'm sure He will be all smiles.

NOTES

1. Lyle W. Dorsett, *A Passion For Souls: The Life of D.L. Moody* (Chicago: Moody Press, 1997), 141.

2. Quoted in William A. Beckham, *The Second Reformation* (Houston: Touch Publications, 1995), 222.

We'd love to have you download our catalog of
titles we publish at:

www.TEACHServices.com

or write or email us your thoughts,
reactions, or criticism about this
or any other book we publish at:

TEACH Services, Inc.
254 Donovan Road
Brushton, NY 12916

info@TEACHServices.com

or you may call us at:

518/358-3494